GOLDEN BOYS

THE GOLDEN STATE WARRIORS' HISTORIC 2015 CHAMPIONSHIP SEASON

Foreword by **JIM BARNETT**

BayArea
NewsGroup

Stephen Curry kisses his daughter, Riley, as he and his teammates celebrate the franchise's first NBA title since 1975. (Nhat V. Meyer/Staff)

This book is book is available in quantity at special discounts for your group
or organization. For further information, contact:

Triumph Books LLC
814 North Franklin Street
Chicago, Illinois 60610
Phone: (312) 337-0747
www.triumphbooks.com

Printed in U.S.A.
ISBN: 978-1-62937-066-8

Bay Area News Group
Sharon Ryan, Publisher and President, Bay Area News Group
David J. Butler, Editor and Vice President for News, MediaNewsGroup
Bert Robinson, Managing Editor, Bay Area News Group
Bud Geracie, Executive Sports Editor, Bay Area News Group

Content packaged by Mojo Media, Inc.
Joe Funk: Editor
Jason Hinman: Creative Director

Front cover photo by Nhat V. Meyer/Staff. Back cover photo by Jose Carlos Fajardo/Staff.

CONTENTS

The regular season MVP, Stephen Curry, can crack a smile after helping the Warriors defeat the Cavaliers in Game 6 of the NBA Finals. (Ray Chavez/Staff)

FOREWORD
BY JIM BARNETT

The Golden State Warriors are the 2015 NBA Champions! The last time that happened was 40 years ago, in 1975. When they won then, Bill King, longtime voice of the Warriors proclaimed, "The Golden State Warriors are champions of the world!"

Yes, the world has changed a lot over the last 40 years. But when you win an NBA championship you do inherit the title of the best basketball team in the world. That has never changed. Yes, the game is different in so many ways; the 3-point line, which is often a deciding factor in many NBA games, being the most obvious. This present day Warriors team used that weapon to achieve their ultimate goal. Present day players are bigger, stronger and quicker than the generation on that 1975 championship team. But the basic fundamentals of the game will never change. Five teammates, playing in harmony to put the ball in the basket at one end of the court, and trying to prevent your opponent from doing the same at the other end is still the objective.

There are so many parallels between that 1975 team and the 2015 version — they seem to intersect often in conversation. Both were dark horses, not even remotely considered to be championship teams at the start of their respective seasons. Both teams depended on role players who came off the bench to play vital roles in helping to win basketball games. They both played selfless team basketball to achieve success. Both teams were blessed with that special chemistry that brings players together to work as one to achieve the goal of a championship.

The Warriors of 40 years ago, led by Rick Barry and coached by Al Attles, won only 48 games in the regular season. They were underdogs in every playoff series. When they persevered to find themselves in the NBA Finals against a heavily favored Washington Bullets team, they shocked everyone by sweeping them 4-0 to win the championship.

This 2015 team won a franchise-record 67 games, a remarkable achievement by any standards. They were led by Stephen Curry, a shooter many call the greatest shooter in the history of the game. It may be hyperbole, but not without some merit as he became the league's MVP. Their achievement was even more astounding as they were led by a rookie head coach in Steve Kerr. Steve won five NBA Championships during his 15-year playing career. His experience had a profoundly positive effect on this rather young, upstart team.

This team quickly became favorites in every series they played. They swept New Orleans, 4-0. They beat a tough Memphis Grizzlies squad, 4-2, after falling behind 2-1 in the first three games. They conquered a very good Houston team with relative ease, 4-1, earning them the title of Western Conference Champions.

As favorites to win the NBA Championship, the Warriors met the Cleveland Cavaliers, a team that had never won a championship during its 45 years in the league. The Cavaliers were led by LeBron James, himself a 4-time league MVP, and accepted as the most dominant player in the NBA. With Curry, the current MVP, and James, it became the most-watched NBA Finals in history.

There were many storylines throughout the series, but it ultimately came down to who could prevail under

Klay Thompson fist bumps a fan prior to Game 1 of the NBA Finals, in which he scored 21 points. (Nhat V. Meyer/Staff)

pressure and execute the best when the game was on the line. LeBron carried his team in the early games of the series, averaging an astonishing 40 points per game. The better-shooting Warriors finally started clicking in Game 4. It became a three-game series with the Warriors holding home-court advantage. The partisan, maniacal Oracle Arena fans bolstered the Warriors confidence. Owning the best home record at 39-2 during the regular season, the Warriors parlayed home-court advantage to their benefit. The Golden State Warriors became the 2015 NBA Champions!

This is a story of a team coming together, blending emerging stars, a few veteran role players and a deep bench, that made it possible to become the best team in the NBA. And this is a team that promises to bring the Bay Area genuine hope in the coming years as well.

For me personally, it is my first experience with a connection to a championship season. Spending 11 years as an NBA player and the last 30 years as the Warriors' television analyst, this season became very special. For that I am grateful. But the most gratifying aspect of this team's achievement is to share in a small way this accomplishment with them. I am genuinely happy for a group of young men who are as outstanding in life off the court as they are when playing the wonderful game of basketball at its highest level. ∎

INTRODUCTION
BY DIAMOND LEUNG

Stephen Curry held the game ball over his head, then handed it to Steve Kerr. And with that, the Warriors players launched a surprise attack, dousing their coach with bottled water.

It was April 4 in Dallas, and there was much to celebrate. The Warriors had run their winning streak to 12, giving Kerr 63 wins, the most ever by an NBA rookie coach. Most importantly, this victory clinched the No. 1 seed for the Warriors, giving them home-court advantage throughout the postseason.

"No championship is won with one guy," Curry said that night. "No championship is won with five guys. Everybody who steps on that floor will be impactful in some way, shape or form. We have guys all over this locker room that can do that."

Curry was right. He himself had gone from a sweet-shooting All-Star to a national icon, ultimately becoming the first Warriors player to win MVP since the franchise moved west in 1962. Through it all he remained family-friendly, humble and unselfish, preferring to highlight how each of his teammates combined to make the Warriors great.

Klay Thompson, Curry's steady and stoic sidekick, was the other half of the historic jump-shooting backcourt and added to its legend with a record-setting 37-point quarter against Sacramento in January. Draymond Green, the fiery third-year player, became the team's heartbeat and its best defender, finishing second in the voting for NBA Defensive Player of the Year.

Andrew Bogut, dogged by injuries in his career, and Harrison Barnes, coming off a troubling season, both shook their problems. Andre Iguodala and David Lee, both former All Stars, accepted bench roles with grace and stepped forward during the championship run.

Shaun Livingston, Leandro Barbosa, Festus Ezeli and Marreese "Mo Buckets" Speights made "Strength in Numbers" more than a marketing slogan.

"I'm grateful to have this team behind me," Curry said during his emotional MVP speech with his teammates on stage alongside him and the trophy. "This is not possible without you guys. I want everybody to get a fingerprint on that so I can remember who I rolled with during this year."

Kerr, a former player and broadcaster, was the Warriors' main offseason addition. He inherited a 51-win team from Mark Jackson and made them a 67-win team by implementing a ball-movement motion offense and holding players to a higher standard.

The Warriors won their first five games, then lost two in a row. The first was a 12-point setback in Phoenix, a game in which Curry committed 10 turnovers. The second was a 13-point drubbing at the hands of the reigning champion San Antonio Spurs.

"We lost to a great team, but we learned," Kerr said.

He was right. The Warriors responded with a 16-game winning streak, the longest in franchise history. Shortly thereafter, they won 13 of 14.

They lost only one more game at home, going 39-2 at Oracle Arena — or Roaracle, as it came to be known. They never lost three games in a row all season, including the playoffs. In a season that spanned more than 100 games, their longest losing streak was two.

There would be comparisons to the 1995-96 Chicago Bulls, a team on which Kerr played alongside Michael Jordan. For a long while, the Warriors remained on that team's 72-win pace. But Kerr downplayed those

After winning three straight NBA Finals games, the Warriors pose for the cameras with the Larry O'Brien trophy. (Jose Carlos Fajardo/Staff)

comparisons, at one point calling them blasphemous. Jordan paid a visit one night, interrupting Kerr's news conference after a victory in Charlotte to hug the first-year coach and tell him to keep up the good work.

He did.

The Warriors rolled through the first round of the playoffs, sweeping the New Orleans Pelicans. Curry averaged 33.8 points per game in the series and delivered a signature moment in Game 3. His three-pointer from the corner, launched while he was falling out of bounds, capped a 20-point fourth-quarter rally and sent the game into overtime.

In the second round, against Memphis, the Warriors lost Games 2 and 3. But instead of losing three straight, they won three straight and moved into the Western Conference finals for the first time since 1975.

Once there, they dispatched of the Houston Rockets and James Harden, the man who had finished second to Curry in the MVP voting. The Warriors got two scares in the series — one when Curry took a terrible fall in Game 4 and the other when Thompson suffered a concussion in Game 5.

In the NBA Finals, they again fell behind 2-1 in the series. Again, they did not lose a third straight game. Instead, despite an historic performance by LeBron James, they won it all. ■

GAME 1

JUNE 4, 2015 • OAKLAND, CALIFORNIA
WARRIORS 108, CAVALIERS 100, OT

LEBRON STRIKES, WARRIORS FINISH

GOLDEN STATE D NEARLY HOLDS CLEVELAND SCORELESS IN OVERTIME

BY DIAMOND LEUNG

Stephen Curry flexed at midcourt after stealing the ball from LeBron James. The Cleveland Cavaliers were sunk after that meeting among MVPs, and Game 1 of the NBA Finals belonged to the Warriors.

The Warriors stood tall in the overtime period of their first Finals game in 40 years, nearly pitching a shutout as part of a memorable defensive stand against James to earn a 108-100 at Oracle Arena on Thursday.

"It was just a classic five minutes that we needed to get that win," Curry said.

For all but the last nine seconds of the five-minute overtime period, the Cavaliers failed to score a single point on a night when James had been dominant during regulation. James could only put his head down and walk off through the tunnel with the final seconds ticking away after having finished with 44 points and the loss.

The Warriors saw the Cavaliers miss their first eight shots of the extra period and allowed only James' meaningless layup with 8.9 seconds left before he disappeared from the scene.

"We really only had zero points," James said.

Curry finished the game with 26 points and eight assists, and his steal with 1:52 left sealed the win. It came after Harrison Barnes' 3-pointer gave the Warriors a 105-98 lead, and the Cavaliers showed no signs they would snap out of their late offensive funk.

The 6-foot-8 James, despite bullying defenders at times on his way to notching his second game of at least 40 points against the Warriors this season, hardly had anything left in the tank after missing in the final seconds of regulation with a chance to win the game.

The Cavaliers also might have suffered another significant blow. Point guard Kyrie Irving, who scored 23 points, left the game in overtime after apparently injuring his knee once again and left the arena on crutches.

Klay Thompson added 21 points after having recovered from a concussion, and Andre Iguodala came off the bench to score 15 points and get key stops on defense going up against James.

The night had seemingly belonged to James, who opened his fifth straight Finals appearance with an 18-for-38 shooting performance, eight rebounds and six assists. Time and time again, he backed down defenders including Barnes, Iguodala, Thompson and Draymond Green for baskets.

But then James misfired on three shots and committed two of his four turnovers in overtime before that final layup in a losing effort ended a stretch of 12

In a battle of superstars, Stephen Curry dishes behind LeBron James during Game 1 of the NBA Finals. (Nhat V. Meyer/Staff)

straight misses for the Cavaliers.

"We had so many opportunities to win this game, and we didn't," James said.

"I don't think I was great."

Cavaliers coach David Blatt was willing to entertain the idea that fatigue was a factor in his team's struggles in overtime. Green said of wearing down James, who played 46 minutes, "That's the plan."

The Warriors, on the other hand, kept fighting.

"It's just the hallmark of this team," Warriors assistant coach Ron Adams said of bouncing back to stop James. "That's who they are. They don't get down. They have obviously a good connectedness as a team, because they always believe they're going to win."

The game went to overtime with the score tied at 98 after James missed a step-back jump shot over Iguodala and Iman Shumpert missed off the rim at the buzzer.

Curry had put the Warriors ahead with a jump shot with 53.6 seconds left in regulation. But Timofey Mozgov calmly hit two free throws to tie it, and Irving blocked Curry on the other end to give the Cavaliers the last shot.

"I didn't even think we were going to have overtime because I thought Iman's follow was going in," Warriors coach Steve Kerr said. "It looked good the whole way. It was right on line."

Curry put on a show in the second quarter as the Warriors shot their way back into the game after trailing by as many as 14 points in the first. He scored the final eight points of a 12-0 run that gave Golden State a 41-36 lead.

Curry's off-balance corner 3-pointer off a give-and-go tied the score at 36, and his steal at midcourt to set up a step-back shot from beyond the arc put the Warriors ahead.

Marreese Speights also gave the Warriors a lift, coming off the bench in his first action after recovering from a calf injury to go 3 for 4 from the field in the second.

James responded, leading an 7-0 run to finish the first half with 19 points.

Besides his defensive effort on James, Iguodala came through with two big dunks that changed the feel of the game.

One came as he was matched up one-on-one with James, who got off-balance and could only watch as he blew by for the jam that closed out the first quarter with the Cavaliers leading 29-19. The other came after he stole the ball from James and then on the other end dunked with 1.5 seconds left in the third to tie the score at 73. ∎

Center Andrew Bogut throws down a dunk during the fourth quarter of Game 1, which the Warriors won in overtime. (Jose Carlos Fajardo/Staff)

A gift for you

Hi Ian, Enjoy your gift and get well soon!
Love, Finn and Debbie

GAME 2

JUNE 7, 2015 • OAKLAND, CALIFORNIA
CAVALIERS 95, WARRIORS 93, OT

NOT SO FAST

CURRY QUIETED AS CAVS STEAL ONE IN OAKLAND

BY DIAMOND LEUNG

Frigid-shooting Stephen Curry's worst playoff performance of his career came in the NBA Finals.

The Warriors made one stirring comeback to send Game 2 into overtime, but a second surge in the extra period fell short, and the final possession ended on a Curry turnover.

And now the series is evened up after undermanned Cleveland survived 95-93 on Sunday at Oracle Arena, holding off the Warriors as LeBron James' triple-double carried the Cavaliers to their first Finals win in franchise history.

"I'm not going to let one game kind of alter my confidence," Curry said. "I know as a team we're not going to let one game alter our belief that we're going to win the series."

Matthew Dellavedova, starting in place of injured All-Star point guard Kyrie Irving, collected an offensive rebound and made two ensuing free throws with 10.1 seconds left in overtime to put the Cavaliers ahead 94-93.

Curry on the other end could only hoist up an air ball, finishing the night with 19 points on 5-for-23 shooting. With the Warriors trailing by two with 4.4 seconds left, Curry had the ball stolen by Iman Shumpert for his sixth turnover.

"I doubt this will happen again," Curry said of his poor game.

Four-time MVP James racked up 39 points, 16 rebounds and 11 assists in 50 minutes on a day when it was the reigning MVP who couldn't get much going despite the Cavaliers missing Irving.

Curry, guarded by Dellavedova for much of the game, proved to be human as he went 2 for 15 from 3-point range.

"It had everything to do with Delly," James said of the Saint Mary's product. "He just kept a body on Steph. He made Steph work. He was spectacular, man, defensively."

Klay Thompson kept the Warriors alive with 34 points but was shut out in overtime as the Warriors lost for only the fourth time at Oracle Arena this season.

After scoring 44 points in a Game 1 overtime loss with little help from his teammates, James got some this time. Timofey Mozgov had 17 points and 11 rebounds. J.R. Smith scored 13 points off the bench. Tristan Thompson grabbed 14 rebounds.

And then there was Dellavedova, who grabbed that key offensive rebound for the Cavaliers' 14th of the game and calmly scored the tying and go-ahead points.

"That is a classic thing you practice as a kid growing up: Down one, you need to make both free throws," Dellavedova said.

Only when Curry got past the defense for a finger-roll to tie the score at 87 with 7.2 seconds left in regulation was he able to do some celebrating. The Warriors finished regulation on a 9-2 run as James missed a layup and Tristan Thompson's tip-in attempt was no good at the buzzer.

But the Warriors were done in by poor shooting, finishing 39.8 percent from the field and 22.9 percent

The Oracle Arena fans react as Matthew Dellavedova, who capably defended Stephen Curry during Game 2, dives for a loose ball. [Jose Carlos Fajardo/Staff]

from 3-point range. Fittingly, Marreese Speights blew a wide-open breakaway dunk attempt at the end of the third quarter.

"Adjust what?" Warriors forward Draymond Green said. "Offense? Making shots? It's hard to adjust making shots."

The Cavaliers were even worse at 32.2 percent overall, but earning the victory in spite of that was a sign of their grittiness, according to James. Cleveland won the rebounding battle 55-45 and scored 15 second-chance points.

"Our guys love the fact that we've been counted out and come into the series being an underdog," James said. "They're pretty much saying that, especially after Kyrie got hurt, that the series was over. I think our guys are using that as motivation."

James was 11 for 35 from the field, with the Cavaliers winning after he missed each of his three attempts in overtime and saw two of them blocked by Green.

"That's why it hurts even more," Klay Thompson said. "I'm proud of the way we all fought."

The Cavaliers led 47-45 at halftime, as Klay Thompson caught fire and scored 20 points to match the first-half total for James.

Thompson was 9 for 13 from the field in the first half, enabling the Warriors to keep the game close despite Curry going 2 for 10, including 1 for 7 from 3-point range.

In the first quarter, Curry scored on a high-arcing reverse layup and then tossed a behind-the-back pass to Leandro Barbosa for a 3-pointer that gave the Warriors a 20-12 lead.

The Cavaliers responded with a 10-0 run, including six points from James, to take the lead. Then they used a 15-2 run powered by an unlikely eight-point contribution from James Jones off the bench to extend the lead to 40-33. ■

GAME 3

JUNE 9, 2015 • CLEVELAND, OHIO
CAVALIERS 96, WARRIORS 91

STAGNANT START

DESPITE LATE WARRIORS RALLY, DELLY, LEBRON PUSH CAVS TO 2-1 SERIES LEAD

BY DIAMOND LEUNG

Once again, the offensively stagnant Warriors were left scratching and shaking their heads after falling short against the Cleveland Cavaliers.

The Cavaliers befuddled the Warriors' juggernaut offense before their home crowd and held off a late charge to escape with a 96-91 win in Game 3 of the NBA Finals on Tuesday to take a 2-1 lead in the best-of seven series.

"I didn't like our energy," Warriors coach Steve Kerr said. "I didn't like our body language for much of that first three quarters. This is what we have to fight through."

The Warriors threatened to come back from a 20-point deficit in the fourth, but there was LeBron James in the end finishing with 40 points, 12 rebounds and eight assists. The Cavaliers are two wins away from the title, and teams that win Game 3 of the Finals with the series tied 1–1 go on to become champions 84 percent of the time.

Stephen Curry scored 17 of his 27 points in the fourth after a sluggish start. But once again, he was outshined by Matthew Dellavedova, who scored 20 points, pestered the MVP on defense and came up with loose ball after loose ball in crunchtime.

Curry hit his seventh 3-pointer to cut the deficit to 94-91 with 18.9 seconds left, and after an inadvertent whistle would have left the Warriors with the ball, the ruling was overturned by a video replay. James, who has embraced an underdog role in the series, finished off the favored Warriors with free throws and led his injury-plagued team to a second straight win.

The Warriors shot 40 percent from the field, and saw Harrison Barnes go scoreless in 19 minutes on 0-for-8 shooting while Draymond Green was 2 for 10 from the field. Green acknowledged afterward he is dealing with a back injury.

The Warriors expressed confidence rather than frustration after a game they never led and yet another slow start they could not explain.

"We haven't even had a good game offensively these three days, and we were still in it every game," guard Klay Thompson said. "If we get our offense back, which we will, we're going to win this series."

Trailing by 17 points at the start of the fourth quarter, the Warriors still roared back and cut the deficit to 79-76 with 5:40 left. The hot start to the quarter was fueled by bench players David Lee, Leandro Barbosa and Andre Iguodala. Curry's reverse layup cut it to three, and then his fourth 3-pointer of the game cut it to 81-80.

"We became the aggressors," Curry said. "For us to win this series, we have to play that way the whole game. We have the depth. We have the talent to do it."

Kerr said: "It was good to see us bring the fight to the game."

Stephen Curry defends LeBron James of the Cavaliers, who won Game 2 despite a 36-point fourth quarter from Golden State. (Nhat V. Meyer/Staff)

But Dellavedova responded with a 3-point play off a one-handed circus bank shot. Curry then threw a behind-the-back pass out of bounds for one of his six turnovers to set up James' 3-pointer to make it 87-80 with 1:44 left.

With the Warriors scrambling after a loose ball and the Cavaliers leading 88-83, it was Dellavedova who made a headlong dive and ended up on the bottom of the pile with the ball as he was fouled.

"Delly! Delly! Delly!" the crowd chanted at the Saint Mary's product who would experience severe cramping after the game and be sent to the hospital for treatment. They were even louder than any "MVP" chant the crowd gave to the four-time award winner James.

The Cavaliers went on a 12-0 run in the third quarter to push the lead to 20 points. It started when Curry committed a turnover and James hit a 3-pointer.

The Warriors trailed 44-37 at halftime, being held to the fewest amount of points in any first half this season. Curry scored only three points in the half on 1-for-6 shooting as the Warriors remained cold from 3-point range with a 3-for-16 start.

"We've just got to continue to put the pressure on them, try to keep them below their averages," James said.

Kerr said: "Steph never loses confidence. I just thought he lost a little energy, and I don't know, life. We just need life from everybody. We need emotion for everybody.

"But we've got to fight through the down periods with just that competitive life and energy." ∎

GAME 4

JUNE 11, 2015 • CLEVELAND, OHIO
WARRIORS 103, CAVALIERS 82

ANDRE THE GIANT

WITH A BOLD MOVE, WARRIORS GET EVEN

BY DIAMOND LEUNG

The Warriors' killer instinct in the NBA Finals is back.

To get the Warriors back on track and even the series with a 103-82 Game 4 rout of the Cleveland Cavaliers, coach Steve Kerr sprang a surprise and used a tactical gambit Thursday.

Desperate for a win and for their high-powered offense to reappear, the Warriors unleashed a starting lineup that included Andre Iguodala for the first time this season and struggling center Andrew Bogut on the bench.

"Boom, Coach Kerr goes to the small lineup, and the complete flow of the game changed," said the Warriors' Draymond Green, who started at center.

"This entire series it's been them as the enforcers, them as the aggressors and us on our heels. We needed to reverse that."

Iguodala gave the Warriors another ballhandler to jump-start their offense and defender to lock down LeBron James, who had scored the most points in Finals history after three games.

Iguodala and Stephen Curry scored 22 points apiece, while a bloodied James was held to 20 points, 12 rebounds and eight assists.

Curry and Iguodala each hit four 3-pointers, and James was 7 for 22 from the field. Timofey Mozgov led all scorers with 28 points, but the Warriors didn't mind, as it was their small lineup that turned the tide.

"It made sense when he told us because we've been getting off to such slow starts," Curry said of Kerr. "When we have that lineup out there in parts of the game, we were able to turn defensive stops into transition and just pick the tempo and the pace of the game up.

"And if we do that from the jump, we thought we'd put pressure on them and not let them be so comfortable with the lead like they've had the last couple games."

Iguodala, whom Kerr called the Warriors' best player in the Finals thus far, led all scorers in the first quarter with nine points as the Warriors took a 31-24 lead.

The Cavaliers scored the first seven points of the game, with James tossing a no-look pass over his shoulder to Mozgov for a dunk and Iman Shumpert hitting a 3-pointer.

But with Green scoring 13 of his 17 points in the first half, the Warriors got an extra burst of energy and controlled the tempo.

Green snapped out of his struggles on offense by scoring on a 3-point play to tie the score at 20, beating his chest in excitement after falling to the floor when he drew the foul on Mozgov. Green celebrated similarly

Rookie head coach Steve Kerr made a deft move in Game 4 by inserting Andre Iguodala into the starting lineup. (Nhat V. Meyer/Staff)

after hitting a 3-pointer to extend the lead to 44-32.

"I'm back," Green screamed.

David Lee, whose impactful Game 3 performance earned him more playing time, became the Warriors' sixth man and was also used at center.

Bogut played only three minutes and said he had no problem with the lineup change, noting that it worked perfectly in a win.

"The whole pride thing, I could really care (less), because if you have a ring at the end of the day, that'll be pride," Bogut said.

Bogut committed three fouls and sent an airborne James sprawling out of bounds, where he cut his head on a camera with 4:43 left in the second quarter.

James, after wrapping a towel over the bloody gash, remained in the game. He later required stitches and complained of a slight headache.

The Cavaliers were held to 33 percent shooting, including 4 for 27 from 3-point range. They won the rebounding battle 49-44 but not decisively enough against the Warriors' small lineup that wreaked havoc.

"Every playoff game is like a precious moment," Iguodala said. "Every possession, every timeout. You've got to be locked in."

Said Curry: "It was about effort and consistent effort every possession."

Iguodala started the second half as well, but the Warriors couldn't keep the momentum.

The Cavaliers went on a 12-2 run capped by James completing an alley-oop from Matthew Dellavedova to cut the Warriors' lead to 65-62.

The Warriors went into the fourth quarter leading 76-70 after Curry's 3-pointer closed out the third. Curry pushed the ball off a rebound and fed Thompson for a layup to make it 80-70. The MVP's runner made it a 12-point lead.

Iguodala's third 3-pointer of the game made it 88-74.

"He's one of the X-factors, and he came to play," James said. ∎

Andre Iguodala sinks one of his four 3-pointers during Game 4. In addition to scoring 22 points, he also limited LeBron James to a 7-of-22 shooting day. (Nhat V. Meyer/Staff)

GAME 5
JUNE 14, 2015 • OAKLAND, CALIFORNIA
WARRIORS 104, CAVALIERS 91

THE RIGHT STEPH
CURRY LIGHTS UP CAVS FROM BEHIND THE ARC
BY DIAMOND LEUNG

Stephen Curry dazzled his defender with ballhandling, stepped back and delivered the dagger as he has done dozens of times this season.

This one in Game 5 of the NBA Finals was different. So meaningful was the shot that it had Curry high-fiving fans in the front row at Oracle Arena. Then for good measure, he sank another one from 29 feet away to seal the win.

The so-called jump-shooting team is just one win away from the NBA championship after Curry led the Warriors to a 104-91 victory against the Cleveland Cavaliers on Sunday that gave them a 3-2 lead in the series.

Curry poured in 37 points, with 17 of them coming in the fourth quarter. His sixth 3-pointer came after tantalizing Matthew Dellavedova with a crossover dribble and gave the Warriors a 96-86 lead with 2:44 left.

"Phew," Warriors forward Draymond Green repeated to emphasize how the play left him breathless. "Phew."

Curry's seventh 3-pointer, coming after the Cavaliers failed to foul him, was a kill shot.

"The show he put on was unbelievable," Warriors guard Klay Thompson said.

Curry was 13 for 23 from the field, including 7 for 13 from 3-point range. The MVP's eruption served as a response to earlier struggles that led to Dellavedova being touted as the one who could stop him.

The barrage overcame LeBron James' big numbers. James notched another triple-double with 40 points, 14 rebounds and 11 assists, but it wasn't nearly enough to beat Curry's sharpshooting.

"I don't know, were any of them not contested, hand in his face, falling, step-back off the dribble?" James said of Curry's shooting.

"I mean, you tip your hat to a guy who makes shots like that, and he's the guy that can do it in our league. He's the best shooter in our league."

Golden State was 12 for 26 from 3-point range, led by Curry, who was slightly dehydrated after the game and returned to the locker room to take in fluids but was expected to be fine for Game 6 on Tuesday in Cleveland, according to a team spokesman.

Green had 16 points, nine rebounds and six assists, getting the Warriors off to a fine start with 10 of their first 14 points. Andre Iguodala, making his second straight start, defended James and had 14 points, eight rebounds and seven assists without committing a turnover.

"He's going to make everyone else on the team great, and at the same time, we're going to help him be great," Iguodala said of Curry.

Thompson, who scored 12 points, raised his index finger as he walked off the court. Later in the locker room, he leaned back in his chair and did it again. One

Stephen Curry goes up for a layup against Tristan Thompson in the fourth quarter, during which he scored 17 points. (Jose Carlos Fajardo/Staff)

more win, and the Warriors have their title.

"We're confident," Curry said, adding that he'd answer a question on whether his 3-pointer over Dellavedova was a signature moment "after we win the championship."

The Cavaliers for a time were able to match the Warriors' pace and finished the quarter tied at 22 as 7-foot-1 Timofey Mozgov was removed from the game early. Tristan Thompson added 19 points for Cleveland, but the center Mozgov was scoreless in nine minutes after leading all scorers in Game 4.

"The reality is this is a small series, and it works well for us," said Warriors coach Steve Kerr, who did not play center Andrew Bogut. "We're comfortable with this style."

Even when using their small lineup, the Warriors deflated the Cavaliers by winning the rebounding battle 43-37. The Warriors also held an 18-3 advantage on fast-break points.

James racked up 20 points, eight rebounds and eight assists in the first half alone to match his scoring total from the Cavaliers' loss in Game 4. Just how dominant was the four-time MVP? Of the Cavaliers' 17 first-half field goals, James either scored or assisted on the last 16 of them.

"If he gets 40, he gets 40," Green said. "But as long as you make him work for those 40, then you've got to be satisfied with what you do."

The Warriors did retake the lead at halftime after Harrison Barnes had a putback dunk while being fouled by James, as the 3-point play put them up 51-50 headed to the locker room.

In the third quarter, Curry and Iguodala hit back-to-back 3-pointers before Leandro Barbosa scored the Warriors' last four points to give them a 73-67 lead heading into the final period. Barbosa finished with 13 points, giving the Warriors a lift off the bench after making his first four field goal attempts.

James gave the Cavaliers the lead with a 34-foot 3-pointer, but then Curry and Klay Thompson struck back with back-to-back 3-pointers to give the Warriors an 85-80 lead.

"We had a lack of effort in a lot of areas in Game 4, and we can't repeat that or they'll raise the trophy for sure," James said. ∎

Harrison Barnes battles Tristan Thompson for a rebound during the fourth quarter of the Warriors' 104–91 victory. (Jose Carlos Fajardo/Staff)

GAME 6

JUNE 16, 2015 • CLEVELAND, OHIO
WARRIORS 105, CAVALIERS 97

'PURE JOY'

TITLE ENDS 40 YEARS OF FUTILITY, MARKS NEW BEGINNING

BY DIAMOND LEUNG

In the end, the Warriors left no doubt.

The Warriors, a complete and consistent team experiencing a dream season, crushed the Cleveland Cavaliers with a methodical 105-97 win in Game 6 of the NBA Finals and found themselves at the pinnacle celebrating a new title.

These Warriors can now be called NBA champions.

Golden State captured its first championship trophy since 1975, using the formula it had relied upon all season long. With the leadership and historic shooting of Stephen Curry and contributions from up and down their roster, the Warriors dazzled teams with the highest-scoring offense. With smarts and toughness, they banded together to form a swarming, top-ranked defense under coach Steve Kerr, a five-time champion as a player who became the first rookie coach to win a title since 1982.

"I think what was probably overlooked all year long was that what really wins is the combination of great offense and great defense," said Kerr, his shirt wet from celebrating with sparkling wine.

"Whether you're shooting threes or twos, it's about the balance. To win a title, you have to be able to make stops."

LeBron James, despite averaging 35.8 points per game in the series for the injury-plagued Cavaliers after a 32-point night, was no match for such an opponent as Cleveland's 51-year major professional sports championship drought continues.

Klay Thompson smiled with the NBA Championship Trophy beside him and pointed at Curry, saying the Warriors are "the best team in the world with the best player in the world."

Curry, who toiled for years and turned around a losing culture, led the Warriors with 25 points and threw the ball toward the heavens as the final buzzer was about to sound. He embraced Kerr and what the coach preached.

"Every decision he made, I think everybody bought into it," Curry said. "Whether you understood it or not, you bought into it. Because he's a champion."

When Kerr stood on the stage at Quicken Loans Arena, the first two players he mentioned were Andre Iguodala and David Lee, former All-Stars who had accepted bench roles in the regular season.

Iguodala ultimately became the Finals MVP after his insertion in the starting lineup turned around the series, and he scored 25 points in the clinching win. Kerr said the award was fitting given all that Iguodala had sacrificed.

Draymond Green, whose indomitable spirit

The MVP of the NBA Finals, Andre Iguodala slams home two of his 25 points in Game 6. (Nhat V. Meyer/Staff)

propelled the team, notched a triple-double with 16 points, 11 rebounds and 10 assists.

"They can still say, 'Oh, he's too small, he's too this, he's too that,'" Green said of the doubters. "They can never take this away from me."

"Ever," added owner Joe Lacob, who had promised to deliver a championship after buying the team in 2010.

Even on a night when Thompson was held to five points and fouled out, the Warriors could not be stopped and showed just how well-rounded they were with what Iguodala called "a team of believers."

The Warriors clinched the championship with a decisive victory much like the ones they had all through a 67-win regular season.

The Warriors dominated the first quarter and led 28-15, with Iguodala serving as the sparkplug in the Warriors' small lineup.

James, who was 13 for 33 from the field, kept coming. He hit a 3-pointer to start an 8-2 run that cut the Warriors' lead to 45-43 at halftime.

"Every time I'd get past (Iguodala), another guy would step up — Draymond Green or whatever the case may be," James said.

The Warriors gave major minutes to Shaun Livingston after Iguodala committed his third foul, as he took on the defensive assignment against James. Leandro Barbosa also played as much in the first half as Thompson, who committed three fouls in 10 minutes.

The Cavaliers took the lead briefly with back-to-back baskets to start the second half, but Harrison Barnes hit his third 3-pointer of the game to put the Warriors back on top. Iguodala had a dunk, and Green hit a 3-pointer to give the Warriors a 53-47 lead.

Then the Warriors ran away from the Cavaliers, pushing the ball in transition off missed shots and turnovers.

More than an hour after the game ended, the usually reserved Thompson returned to the locker room and screamed.

"We won the championship! We did it!" ∎

The best team all year long, the Warriors, who went 67-15 during the regular season, cap 2015 by winning the Larry O'Brien trophy. (Jose Carlos Fajardo/Staff)

ANDRE IGUODALA

MVP CHANGED DIRECTION OF FINALS

BY JEFF FARAUDO

Andre Iguodala wasn't a starter all year, but in the biggest game of his life he proved to be a spectacular finisher.

Iguodala scored a season-high 25 points and was named the Most Valuable Player of the NBA Finals as the Warriors held off the Cleveland Cavaliers 105-97 on Tuesday night to win their first world championship in 40 years.

"Unreal," Iguodala said afterward.

Certainly his path to an NBA title in his 11th season was unlikely. A starter in all 758 games his first 10 years, Iguodala was asked during training camp to come off the bench for the benefit of his team.

"For us, it's really fitting for Andre to win the award because he sacrificed his starting role to make Harrison (Barnes) better, to make our bench better," coach Steve Kerr said. "That set the tone for our entire season and everything we were able to accomplish.

"It couldn't happen to a better person."

Iguodala said he couldn't really digest winning the MVP.

"I'm not even thinking about anything. My mind is blank," he said. "I'm enjoying the moment, celebrating with my teammates. Those are the things you remember the most.

"I'm just happy winning the ring. I didn't really care about anything else."

After the Cavaliers won Games 2 and 3, Kerr made a bold change, putting Iguodala back into the starting lineup. And the series turned.

"He saved this season for us," teammate Draymond Green said.

"He turned the ship for us," Shaun Livingston said.

Not only did he shoulder the burden of defending LeBron James, but Iguodala averaged 20.3 points over the final three games as the Warriors sprinted to their title.

Teammate Stephen Curry, the NBA's regular-season MVP, was thrilled for Iguodala.

"Obviously he deserves that Finals MVP for the way he impacted the game at both ends," Curry said. "He just needed an opportunity to show the world. He's a huge reason why we're celebrating."

"Andre is that guy that we all look to when everything's going bad," Green said. "People try to give me credit for being a leader, but we all look to Andre."

Klay Thompson called Iguodala the ultimate professional.

"Never complains," Thompson said. "He's accepted his role like a true pro, and man he stepped up when we needed him."

They needed him on a nightly basis against James, who averaged 35.8 points in the Finals. No one else had the experience, the savvy or the muscle to stand up to James. Livingston called it "the hardest job on the floor."

"Exhausting," explained Iguodala, who has guarded James his entire career. "LeBron doesn't have any glaring weakness, so you've got to pick up on the subtle stuff. It's 11 years picking up all this information."

The first NBA Finals MVP not to start every game in the series, Andre Iguodala receives the MVP award from NBA legend Bill Russell, who grew up in Oakland. (Nhat V. Meyer/Staff)

On Tuesday night, Iguodala added five rebounds, five assists and two steals as Warriors forged a 15-point lead entering the final five minutes of the fourth quarter.

Then, two nights after Iguodala made just two of 11 free throws, Kerr took him off the floor with 3:40 left to prevent the Cavaliers from intentionally fouling him. The Cavs rallied and with 1:50 left, Kerr sent Iguodala back into the game.

After Cleveland fought within four points, Iguodala grabbed two key rebounds in the final 21 seconds and was fouled both times. He made one of two free throws each time, helping to clinch the victory.

All series, Cleveland's defense was geared to minimizing the 3-point capabilities of Curry and Thompson. Others were left open, including Iguodala, who averaged just 7.8 points in the regular season then more than doubled that to 16.0 in the Finals.

"Their plan was to take Steph away and take Klay away and force Andre to beat them," Kerr said. "And he did." ∎

THE
REGULAR
SEASON

Stephen Curry runs on to the court at Oracle Arena prior to the Warriors' home opener against the Lakers. (Anda Chu/Staff)

THE FURY INSIDE

STEVE KERR'S NICE-GUY DEMEANOR MASKS THE INTENSITY THAT SUSTAINED HIS NBA CAREER

BY DIAMOND LEUNG • NOVEMBER 4, 2014

Warriors coach Steve Kerr smiles as he peels away at his nice-guy image, reciting a line his wife half-jokingly uses to describe him around the house. "Beware the fury of a patient man," the even-keeled Kerr said, laughing about occasionally losing his temper.

Bubbling inside the rookie coach is a toughness of character that Warriors staff members who know him best believe will enable success as he has taken over for Mark Jackson on the bench with a 3-0 record heading into Wednesday's game against the rival Los Angeles Clippers.

It's a quality the 49-year-old Kerr revealed when, as a skinny 6-foot-3 shooting guard, he won three championships with the Chicago Bulls playing for Phil Jackson and two with the San Antonio Spurs under Gregg Popovich. Lacking the athleticism to dunk and barely recruited before landing at the University of Arizona, Kerr scraped together a 15-year NBA playing career and worked to become the most accurate 3-point shooter in league history. He once got into a fistfight in practice with Michael Jordan and earned so much respect for it that the following season his famous teammate passed to him for the championship-clinching shot.

"The first time I played in the NBA, I was alarmed by the speed," Kerr said. "The first time I was a broadcaster for TNT, I didn't know which monitor to look at. You've got to feel it."

Making the Rounds

So after leaving television to accept a five-year coaching contract worth up to $25 million, Kerr flew as far as Melbourne, Australia, to dine with center Andrew Bogut and his girlfriend, traveled to Miami to sit with forward Harrison Barnes and his agent, and played rounds of golf with Stephen Curry.

The All-Star Curry was among the players to disagree with Jackson's dismissal in May after back-to-back playoff appearances, but he has repeatedly said Kerr — the son of university educators — did his homework and was detail-oriented in preparing for the job ahead.

Secure in his basketball intellect, Kerr thirsted for more knowledge and surrounded himself with assistant coaches — Alvin Gentry and Ron Adams — who could provide advice culled from the decades of NBA coaching experience he lacked. Kerr proceeded to go to Las Vegas to lead the Warriors' summer league team, a task often left to an assistant.

It was then that Kerr discovered he didn't know how to effectively use a white board.

"I had a bunch of plays in my head, but I didn't communicate them very well," Kerr said. "And so over a two-week stretch in Vegas, I figured out, 'Oh man, I better practice this stuff.' So I spent the rest of the summer literally drawing up plays at the office."

More recently, the sight of a white board on the wall of Kerr's office filled with philosophies and X's and

Motioning to his team in the fourth quarter of Game 5 of the Western Conference Finals, Steve Kerr had a magnificent campaign in his first year as head coach. (Doug Duran/Staff)

O's grabbed the attention of general manager Bob Myers, who was impressed by the preparation work. Kerr and Gentry had collaborated to draw up plays for after-timeout, buzzer-beater, end-of-game and two-for-one situations.

Kerr installed an offense based on ball movement, and from the first to the last day of training camp asked his players to make individual sacrifices for the good of the team. He ordered the removal of panels honoring players who had made the All-Star team that lined an entire wall of the practice facility and replaced them with more team-oriented images. Also taken down was signage celebrating Curry's NBA record-setting 272 3-pointers during the 2012-13 season.

In turn, Kerr, who has spoken of having nerves at the start of his coaching career, seeks input and weighs opinions before making decisions. Curry confirmed that Kerr was comfortable taking suggestions on strategy from players.

"Just knowing his operating modality, I think he may be the smartest guy in the room, but he never acts like the smartest guy in the room," said team President Rick Welts, who was in the same position in Phoenix for the three years when Kerr was general manager.

Humor Helps

In the film room, Kerr routinely shows his sense of humor. After digital content assistant Michael Leslie humorously showed up to work on Halloween dressed in Kerr's Bulls jersey and shorts, the coach had his look-alike make a second surprise entrance at a film session and deliver a few lines of the presentation in front of the team.

Players said the sessions will sometimes include jokes at their expense — say, a lowlight on the tape interrupted by a "Saturday Night Live" cutaway gag — that leaves the team laughing.

The lightheartedness that accompanies the teaching breaks up the monotony to make serious work more enjoyable and serves another useful purpose.

"It gives you a little piece of him," said assistant coach of player development Bruce Fraser, a longtime friend who was Kerr's teammate at Arizona.

"He is who he is. He's not trying to be something he's not, and he's not going to fake that. He's authentic to his core, and when players realize that a guy's real, and he's in it for them and the whole, then that's a powerful thing."

Kerr said the piece of advice he received most was to simply be himself at a time when he was admittedly still finding his voice as a coach. He spoke with brash hall of fame NFL coach Bill Parcells about how to handle players before deciding to take the Warriors job. Kerr sometimes allows for upbeat music to be played during practice, taking a page from fun-loving Pete Carroll of the Seattle Seahawks after attending a training camp session led by the Super Bowl champion coach.

Well-Read Coach

Seeking to stimulate his mind, Kerr has public relations staffers suggest non-basketball articles for his bedtime reading as his special assistant, Nick U'Ren, prints one and lays it in his chair every morning for him to take home.

In a book about the late Arthur Ashe, Kerr read of "the fury of a patient man," a 17th century line of verse that the soft-spoken tennis champion said was one of his favorites. It ultimately became a popular saying in the Kerr family household and now rings true in his new workplace.

"He's let us have it a few times in practice as well when he senses we're not focused," Curry said.

"Hey, don't underestimate that pretty little boy face, OK?" said grinning associate head coach Gentry, who previously worked for Kerr as the head coach in Phoenix.

Fraser, who in college alongside Kerr spoke of one day coaching together, contends the Warriors have only seen glimpses.

"You don't play in the league for as long as he's played in the league with his athleticism and size unless you have something in you, and he has it in him," Fraser said. "He's actually a lot tougher than you would think. He's mild-mannered on the outside and has a fury inside.

"It's in him. It's in him." ■

Two great shooters, Stephen Curry and Steve Kerr, chat during practice before Game 1 of the NBA Finals. (D. Ross Cameron/staff)

11

KLAY THOMPSON

THOMPSON LITERALLY COULDN'T MISS IN RECORD-BREAKING THIRD QUARTER

BY DIAMOND LEUNG • JANUARY 25, 2015

Those who attended the Warriors game against the Sacramento Kings at Oracle Arena witnessed history: Klay Thompson scored 37 points in one quarter, an NBA record, en route to 52 points in a 126-101 victory.

From those who experienced it firsthand Friday night, we recount how it went down, shot by shot, as Thompson lifted the Warriors from a fog that had resulted in an 18-point lead being whittled to 56-51 at halftime.

WARRIORS COACH STEVE KERR: "At halftime, I was so angry I told the guys, 'Run whatever you want.' Like, 'I'm not calling any plays because it's not about any plays we call. It's: Are we going to decide to focus? So run whatever you want.' As (associate head coach Alvin Gentry) would say, they ran two plays: get the ball to Klay, and Klay get the ball."

WARRIORS FORWARD DRAYMOND GREEN: "When he hit the first (3-pointer), it's like, 'Oh, OK. Good.' We went up (three) when he hit the first one. Like, 'Oh, Klay just got us out of the barn.'"

WARRIORS GUARD STEPHEN CURRY: "The first three were shots he normally takes. Just coming down, and he's got a rhythm. And from then on, it was

just finding a glimmer of daylight to get a shot off."

Thompson, with a shot he would later tell KNBR was his first "heat check," hit his fourth 3-pointer of the quarter from about 28 feet over Nik Stauskas to give the Warriors a 74-66 lead.

BOB FITZGERALD ON THE CSNBA BROADCAST: "He shot it from Piedmont. Oh, man!"

TIM ROYE ON THE KNBR BROADCAST: "Heat check confirmed."

TOM TOLBERT ON KNBR: "Fi-yah."

CURRY: "He just pulled up and made it. After that, it was just get him the ball any way we could. Abandon any play sets that we usually run, and either a pindown or just try to get him the ball and make a play, and the rest was history."

Thompson, off a post-up, fed Green for a layup to give the Warriors a 79-68 lead.

GREEN: "I got me a layup in. I know y'all caught that. But if you shoot the ball at that point, you'd get booed. I mean, I was right there, so I had to shoot it. But if I was anywhere else, I would have passed the ball right back to him. He did get an assist."

CURRY: "They knew at a certain point all we were doing was dribbling around trying to get him the ball

Klay Thompson dunks the ball against the Sacramento Kings during the Jan. 25 game when he scored an NBA-record 37 points in one quarter. (Jose Carlos Fajardo/Staff)

like Will Smith in 'Fresh Prince.' Just dribble around, give him the ball, and let him shoot, and they still couldn't get there fast enough. His release was beautiful."

KINGS COACH TYRONE CORBIN: "We came out, closed out, hands down a little bit, and he was getting them off. We tried to double him, but he was getting them off so quickly we couldn't get any help to him."

KINGS CENTER DEMARCUS COUSINS: "It happened so fast there wasn't any time to really think about it. When a guy gets hot like that, with the ball barely touching his fingertips when he is releasing, you can't really stop something like that."

Thompson then saw a 3-point attempt go off the front of the rim, off the backboard and through to make it 82-70 for his sixth 3-pointer of the quarter.

THOMPSON: "I made the one off the curl, and it bounced in. That was a shooter's roll."

TOLBERT: "I want Klay Thompson to go to Cache Creek with me after the game."

Thompson, in front of the Kings bench, heaved the ball up and made his eighth straight 3-pointer of the quarter to make it 92-70.

ROYE: "It had no business going in, but it did! That was just sick!"

THOMPSON: "The one in the corner when my feet were all jacked up. It was off balance, and I just kind of threw it up there."

KERR: "After he made about seven or eight in a row, I was just watching his face just to see what I could see, and I've never seen anybody that zoned in. It was just spectacular to watch."

Thompson with 4.9 seconds left in the third quarter made two free throws after hitting a shot that didn't count after the whistle from 3-point range.

KERR: "(Assistant coach) Jarron Collins turned to me and said, 'We've got to get more balance out of our offense.'"

The quarter ended with Thompson reaching 50 points for the game.

KERR: "I was turning to a couple of the players, and I said, 'Do I get him out?' L.B. (Leandro Barbosa) looked at me. He said, 'No, man. No. Keep him out there.' So we kept him out there and drew up a play for him that didn't work. That's the one he missed (with 9:52 left), and then I got out of the way again. He was gassed at that point. We wanted to give him another couple minutes, and he was just on such a roll. You don't want to break that, but the spell was finally broken, and we got him out, and he got that beautiful ovation."

CURRY: "He said the last three he took, he was dead tired. He was like, 'I know you scored 54 two years ago, and I just wanted to sling that last one up and see if I could make it and get 55.' So he was having fun with that, knowing exactly once he kind of came to and seen what he had done just how special of a night it was. I then told him it took me 48 minutes (to score 54). His points per minute (52 in 33 minutes), that's just unheard of."

GREEN: "I'm honored to be out on the floor just to witness that."

CSNBA SIDELINE REPORTER ROSALYN GOLD-ONWUDE: "Before the (postgame) interview he said, 'That was crazy, Ros, like I blacked out. Crazy, crazy.'"

THOMPSON TO CSN AFTER THE GAME: "It's crazy. I don't really know what happened."

WARRIORS EXECUTIVE JERRY WEST: "I flew back (to his home in Los Angeles) after the game, and honestly, I couldn't go to sleep, " West said Saturday. "I was replaying in my own mind what I had just witnessed. It was incredible to watch. It's something no one's watched, to be honest with you."

More from West, one of the staunchest supporters of keeping Thompson and not trading him for Kevin Love: "They would have had one less employee if that would have happened." ■

Klay Thompson maneuvers between Sacramento's Nik Stauskas (left) and Rudy Gay. Thompson led the Warriors with 52 points in the win, including 37 in the third quarter. (Dan Honda/Staff)

CURRY BRAND

HE'S STILL STEPHEN AT HOME. BABY FACED ASSASSIN ON THE COURT. BUT WITH NEWFOUND STAR POWER.

BY MARCUS THOMPSON II • FEBRUARY 11, 2015

Stephen Curry is on a balcony of his Orinda home, the shadow of his hoodie hides the shiner under his right eye.

He's got a putter in his hand, staring down at a cup on the practice green he had installed. His dog, Reza, faces the lake across the street while watching guard from the balcony. It's in this moment, as he explains ... it becomes so clear.

Curry is actually pretty boring.

"I'm a homebody," Curry said. "I like to keep things simple. I value the time with my family. That's what matters most to me."

And that's been the most difficult part of Curry's broadband-speed rise to stardom. Suddenly, the low-frills Charlotte boy who finds bliss in Chick-fil-A and carpet time with his toddler, is an international star. And the brighter he shines the harder it is for him to find the time to enjoy the humdrum existence.

Curry has become a trio of personas, and managing them is a task nearly even more difficult than beating a double-team off the dribble.

At the core is Stephen, the simple guy-next-door type. On the court is the Baby Faced Assassin, a dazzling point guard whose desire to dominate contradicts his meek appearance.

That's the character the Warriors need Wednesday night against an improving Minnesota squad. Running

on fumes, the Warriors will need a big game from their star if they want to go into the All-Star break with a win.

And then after the game, when he takes a postgame flight to New York for All-Star Weekend, the new character kicks in: Mr. Curry. The celebrity. The spokesman. The brand.

That's who was supposed to be at the video shoot for his signature Under Armour shoe. Mr. Curry was the reason for the whole setup in Los Angeles. The commercial he was filming was a testament to how much clout he's gained.

But that Stephen fella couldn't stop tripping out over Jamie Foxx. Curry was given some options for stars to be in his video and he said Foxx was his top choice. And the megastar agreed.

"That whole experience was crazy," Curry said. "Watching him act and talk about me and my shoe. All I had to do really was shoot during the prediction. So I was literally just watching him the whole time and just in awe."

Last year, Curry made his first All-Star team. This year, he's the top vote-getter and he's throwing his own party — hosted by Foxx — to officially release his new shoe.

When Curry steps off that plane, it will be as the face of Under Armour, the brand ambassador for Express closing, a pitchman for Degree deodorant, State

Hair artist Derek Hernandez, owner of DTB "Derek Tha Barber" at Antioch's Ajja's Barber Shop, poses after finishing cutting the image of Golden State Warrior star Stephen Curry into the hair of Johnny Fernandez, 21, on April 8. Hernandez was featured in an episode of the new reality TV series "Cedric's Barber Battle". (Dan Rosenstrauch/Staff)

Farm Insurance, Footlocker, and Kaiser Permanente.

Don't be fooled. Curry likes his fame. Unlike LeBron James and Kobe Bryant, child prodigies who have been national stars since they were teens, Curry is new to the superstar scene. He's getting access and opportunities that weren't possible two years ago.

The coolest thing Curry said he's done was present at the 2014 Kids' Choice Awards. That was because his family could enjoy it, too. His daughter, Riley, got to see some Nickelodeon characters backstage. And his wife, Ayesha, who grew up with actress aspirations, had that particular award show on her bucket list.

"She might've been a little salty that I was who they invited," Curry said, bursting into laughter.

One of the perks of Curry's status is the clout. It felt odd initially — especially considering how often he uses the words "Yes, dear" — but Curry is getting comfortable exercising the pull he has.

Previously, he wouldn't say anything remotely controversial. But after earning his first All-Star bid, Curry started using his pull.

He pitched in for the recruiting of Dwight Howard during the summer of 2013. Last spring, he lobbied repeatedly for then-coach Mark Jackson. He also spoke out against Donald Sterling and planned a boycott behind the scenes.

When Jackson was fired, sources say Curry was furious in a players-only online group chat. Instead of spouting the company line, he made his disappointment clear when asked.

"I still think they shouldn't have fired Jackson," Curry said, "but I also think they picked the right guy to replace him."

Curry put in his two cents on the Kevin Love-Klay Thompson trade talks the Warriors weighed last summer.

How does that matter moving forward? Stephen, the mild-mannered family guy, isn't the only one calling shots anymore. Mr. Curry is in the picture, and he has all kind of options in his reach. ∎

Stephen Curry writes the Bible quote "I can do all things" on his Under Armour shoes, as seen in this photo taken during the Warriors' win over Memphis on April 13. (Jose Carlos Fajardo/Staff)

WARRIORS CHAMPS LIKE CURRENT TEAM'S CHANCES

FRANCHISE'S LONE TITLE WINNERS PULLING FOR ANOTHER CHAMPIONSHIP

BY CARL STEWARD • MARCH 24, 2015

Jamaal Wilkes really likes those Smash Brothers. Clifford Ray, meanwhile, is quite fond of those Slash Brothers.

Ah, well, you can't hold it against the guys who won the Bay Area's only NBA championship four decades ago to be up on the current nicknames. Smash or slash or splash, they nonetheless like what they see from the latest Warriors model looking to match what they did in 1974-75.

The Warriors brought back seven members of that title team Monday night, along with coaches Al Attles and Joe Roberts and even trainer Dick D'Oliva and publicist Hal Childs, to be honored for delivering the only championship banner hanging at Oracle Arena. The crowd gave them a rousing standing ovation between the first and second quarters.

Before the game, led as usual by their ever-loquacious star Rick Barry, the vintage Warriors told some choice stories from the old days but were just as excited to discuss the current club and the opportunity it has over the next few months.

"I just hope that they stay healthy, because I think they have a real legitimate shot at bringing the second world championship to the Golden State Warriors," Barry said. "I hope that happens for the sake of the organization and the fans as well."

The last time Barry was at Oracle in March 2012, he tried to introduce then-new owner Joe Lacob to a booing crowd on the night of Chris Mullin's number retirement. Barry scolded the fans, who were upset with Lacob over the trade of Monta Ellis, and he got in another good admonishment on this night.

"This is a first-class operation, and I've said all of those fools that were booing during the Chris Mullin special awards ceremony should be writing letters and apologizing to Joe Lacob for what they did," Barry said. "Because it worked out pretty good."

Ray, who anchored the '74-75 team as their hardworking center, said that while the teams are quite different, the current cast seems to embody a similar collective spirit.

"One of the reasons we like this team over all the other Warriors teams that have been down the pike the last 40 years is the feeling they give off and transmit," Ray said. "I feel like this young team has some of the same characteristics we had. I know we all are pulling for them that they're able to complete an outstanding season."

Wilkes was a rookie on the '74-75 team after a great career at UCLA but wasn't inducted into the Basketball Hall of Fame until three years ago. He doesn't make it to the Bay Area much, but even if he got the nickname

Jamaal Wilkes (then known as Keith Wilkes) shoots over Elvin Hayes of the Washington Bullets during Game 3 of the 1975 NBA Finals. (AP Images)

wrong, it's clear he's still paying close attention to the Warriors, particularly guards Stephen Curry and Klay Thompson.

"I think they are two outstanding young players, surrounded by other good players," Wilkes said. "It's a team game, and it takes more than one or two guys. But I think Steph may be approaching Rick Barry status. I don't think he's quite there yet, but he's an incredible talent. And Klay is only going to get better. The thing I like about Klay is not only his shooting, but his defense."

Barry, who said in a recent Sirius radio interview he didn't necessarily consider Curry one of the greatest shooters of all-time, was full of praise for the Warriors point guard on this night, with a few minor quibbles about some of his passes and shot choices.

"But he's really become a great player," Barry said. "Right now, if I had a vote for the MVP, Steph is right there. He's been unbelievable, and the thing I like about him is he's willing to score in the teens — 12, 14, 18 points — and get

Members of the 1974-75 Golden State Warriors team that won the franchise's only NBA championship wave to the crowd during an in-game ceremony commemorating the 40th anniversary of the championship on March 23, 2015. [D. Ross Cameron/Staff]

nine, 10, 12, 15 assists. So he's playing a well-rounded game."

Barry said forward Draymond Green is a "very important part of this team" and singled out former All-Stars David Lee and Andre Iguodala for accepting bench roles.

"It's just awesome," he said. "That's why this is a special team that they have. They're committed to defense, they're a great offensive team, and they're selfless. Great combination."

Barry said his biggest concern about the club's chances in the postseason is how the NBA game becomes more needlessly rugged.

"The only thing you have to be careful about in the playoffs is don't get caught up in the playoff NBA beat-the-(bleep)-out-of-each-other basketball and slow down," he said. "They have to impose their will on the other team and play the way they're capable of playing when they're playing their best. I'm sure Steve (Kerr) is aware of that, so they have to rebound and push the ball and play Warriors basketball and not get caught up in that nonsense." ■

30
STEPHEN CURRY

CURRY BEFRIENDS TEENS WHO ISSUED CHALLENGE ON YOUTH'S HOME COURT

BY DANIEL BROWN • APRIL 17, 2015

For once, the odds were against Stephen Curry making a shot. Jeff Lorenz's mom cautioned the boys more than once that Curry might not show up at all.

She told the kids that the Warriors star might have better things to do than goof around with a bunch of teenagers 2,900 miles from home. But not long after her umpteenth warning, Jeff spotted a car making the slow turn up the family driveway.

Some of the boys kept watching, figuring there must be a luxury vehicle to follow. But there was no limo. Curry and his buddies were all packed into that Mazda 3.

Curry had made his way to central New Jersey after receiving a dare from a couple of bored but gutsy high school students. They videotaped themselves making a trick shot — an improbable heave off a deck from behind the backboard — and wondered if the NBA's famed sharpshooter had the mettle to give it a go himself.

Of course, he did. And the ensuing 2012 journey left behind two lasting lessons for anyone gearing up to watch the Warriors' playoff run that begins Saturday with a home game against the New Orleans Pelicans.

Lesson 1: Curry can drain a shot from anywhere, including a stranger's balcony in Pennington, New Jersey.

Lesson 2: No matter how big the league's MVP candidate gets, he's still the type of guy you want over for pizza and game night.

"I actually beat him in Ping-Pong," Jeff Lorenz, 17, says now. "So I have that over him."

In fairness, it was Curry who laid down the initial challenge. An early adopter of using social media to connect with fans, he staged a contest asking his followers to send him a clip of their most creative backyard trick shot.

The winner would get a nifty prize: Curry would record their outgoing voice mail message. That's why when you call Lorenz now, you hear the point guard's voice instead: "Hi, this is Steph Curry of the Golden State Warriors. If you're trying to reach Jeff, he's not here — probably because we're in the gym shooting hoops. Please leave a message."

When the high school senior calls back, you get the rest of the story: After winning the contest, Jeff's friend Ben Schragger figured out that the Warriors would soon be on a road trip to Philadelphia, with a day off before the game. So they sent an email through Curry's social media team inviting the point guard to come try the shot himself.

"I remember thinking, 'Wow, this kid has a lot of guts,'" recalled Bill Voth, the co-founder of Spiracle Media. "I told him it was very, very unlikely. But when I ran it by Steph, he really didn't even hesitate."

Stephen Curry raises the hardware after leading his team to a series victory in the Western Conference Finals. (Dan Honda/Staff)

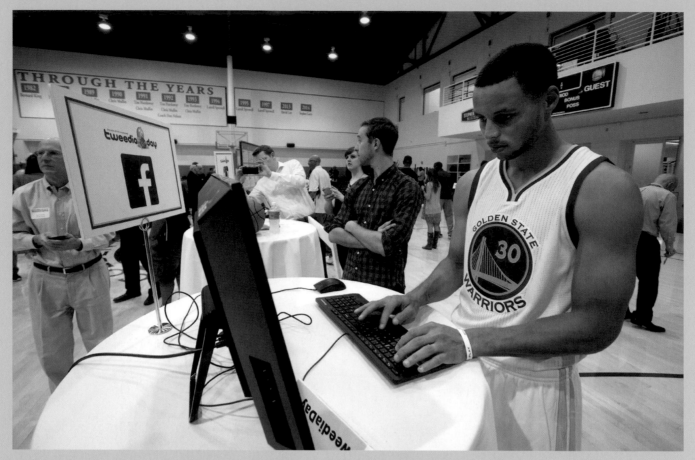

Stephen Curry tweets to fans during the Warriors' media day in September 2014. Curry, who has more than 2.4 million Twitter followers, was an early adopter of social media. (D. Ross Cameron/Staff)

Curry isn't one to run from a shot. On Tuesday, shortly after hitting 77 consecutive three-pointers after practice — and 94 out of 100 overall — he explained why he would go so far out of his way to pal around with freshmen from Hopewell Valley Central High School.

"Just a way to make the world smaller," Curry shrugged. "Obviously, basketball touches a lot of different areas. It's meant a lot to me to have some people in northwestern New Jersey that I can connect with. To be able to involve the fans and make it personal — that's what it's all about."

At the time of his visit, in March 2012, Curry was struggling with the ankle injuries that sidelined him for all but 23 games that season. "I'm like, well, I've got nothing to do on that off-day. So let's go," he recalled.

So he went. And then he stayed. With his social media team on hand to document the trip, they made the 45-minute drive east from Philadelphia to Pennington (pop. 2,600).

It took Curry all of nine tries to knock down the shot,

burying the 35-footer off the 30-foot-high balcony and raising both hands in triumph.

He hadn't come all that way to miss. This was the kind of thing he used to do in his own backyard, inventing games to play against his father, former NBA Sixth Man of the Year winner Dell Curry, and his younger brother, Seth, who currently plays in the NBA Development League.

"On every court, we'd find some weird angle, some crazy shot that had nothing to do with traditional basketball. But when you're a kid and you have that kind of imagination, it's kind of fun," Curry said.

Something about hitting the shot off the balcony that day must have awakened his inner child, because he was on the next game. Curry stuck around to play the shooting contest "knockout," then played Ping-Pong, ate pizza, held a cameras-off Q&A and signed everything not bolted down.

"It was almost as if he went to our school and he was just another kid," Schragger said.

In March 2012 Stephen Curry visited the Penninington, New Jersey home of Jeff Lorenz, then a high school freshman, after Lorenz won a contest Curry staged on social media. Curry spent several hours with Lorenz and his friends, burying a shot from the Lorenz family's balcony, playing a game of "knockout" with the youngsters and posing for photos with the group. Each year when Curry and the Warriors return to Philadelphia, the Warriors star leaves 10 postgame passes for Lorenz and his friends. (Top left and bottom photos courtesy of Ben Schragger, top right photo courtesy of the Lorenz family)

Spiracle Media had asked Lorenz to limit his invite list to six or seven friends. But word got out at school and there were nearly 30 on hand. Curry saw the overflow turnout and was excited, rather than irritated. Voth, his handler that day, considered whisking Curry out of there after a while but never sensed his client wanted to go.

"He's kind of like the anti-NBA player. It wasn't like he was going to go out clubbing or hitting the town," Voth said. "The only thing he had to do that night was to go back to the hotel and FaceTime with his wife."

All along, Lynn Lorenz watched in wonder.

"I couldn't believe it when (Curry) actually showed up," she said. "He is the most unbelievably nice, down-to-earth guy. We're all such huge Steph Curry fans now. I never liked basketball. But now I'm always watching the Warriors because of Steph Curry and what he did for the kids."

In a way, the pizza party rolls on. On every subsequent trip to Philadelphia, Curry arranges for 10 postgame passes for the boys. They show up in homemade "SC30" shirts — that's the name of his monthly contest — and Curry gives them a nod during warm-ups and chats with them after the game.

The kids' story gets better every year. At the time of their first meeting, Curry was a promising youngster best known for his March Madness exploits while at tiny Davidson College in North Carolina.

Now, he's among the famous faces in the NBA, with jersey sales that trail only LeBron James of the Cleveland Cavaliers. This year, Curry broke his own league record with 286 three-pointers while averaging 23.8 points and 7.7 assists for the best team in the NBA.

"Now, everyone says, 'You're the one who knows Steph Curry,'" said Jeff Lorenz. "Because now everybody knows him, even my nonbasketball fans. He's all over the place now. He's got all the commercials. It's just crazy."

Curry this week said he stays in touch with the kids because he likes that the two ringleaders, Jeff and Ben, are into charity work. Jeff does tutoring for the youth organization Urban Promise while Ben is the CEO of the national charity Cards2Kids, which donates sports cards to kids in need.

"They're awesome. They're down-to-earth kids," Curry said. "I know they're hardworking. They have big hearts, too. They do a great job of using whatever platform they have to help others.

"They're pretty good at Ping-Pong, too. They kind of beat me up when I went over to their house." ■

Opposite: Stephen Curry and wife Ayesha pose for photographs while helping to hand out food to needy families at Oakland's Beebe Memorial Cathedral. (D. Ross Cameron/Staff)

23
DRAYMOND GREEN

INTENSE GREEN'S EMOTIONAL FIRE BIG PART OF HIS SKILL SET

BY JEFF FARAUDO • APRIL 22, 2015

Early this season, as Draymond Green still was getting to know the Warriors' new coach, he barked at Steve Kerr on the sideline during a game, then worried he had crossed the line.

"I walked up to him and said, 'My bad.' And he's like, 'You're good. I love that fire,'" Green recalled.

Well, the fire has been unleashed, and the Warriors — up 2-0 in their first-round NBA playoff series against the New Orleans Pelicans — are far better for it.

"I love it. I love the edge. I love the passion," Kerr said. "We both know we're in the same fight together and we're coming from maybe two different perspectives, but with the same goal. It's healthy and it's fun."

Green gave a nationwide TNT audience a look at the full range of his skills — and his bark — in the Warriors' 97-87 win over New Orleans in Game 2 on Monday.

Player and coach had words after Kerr pulled Green from the game to give him a rest with 3:55 left in the first quarter.

"I was over there hot," Green said afterward. The two sorted things out and Green was back on the floor 3 minutes later.

Green wound up with 14 points, 12 rebounds, five assists, three steals and two blocked shots, and outplayed young Pelicans superstar Anthony Davis in the fourth quarter, allowing the Warriors to pull away. All this despite spraining his left ankle twice during the game.

"You have to have guys who can put up a fight," Kerr said afterward, "and Draymond put up an incredible fight."

Kerr acknowledges he had no idea what he was getting with Green when he took the job. He imagined, in fact, that David Lee would retain the power forward job as soon as he was healthy, and expected the two might share minutes.

"I really didn't anticipate him seizing the position," Kerr said. "That's all him. That's his effort and his impact on the team."

The impact is best defined by Green's relentless intensity. Ask Green and he'll tell you it's much more than an attitude. It's a skill.

"Take Steph's handles away from him, I don't think he'll be that same player," Green said of teammate Stephen Curry's ballhandling. "That's just a part of who I am. I play with a lot of intensity. That's a skill, to play with the intensity I play with."

Draymond Green goes up for a shot against Cleveland in the second quarter of Game 1 of the NBA Finals. Green was the Warriors' third leading scorer during the regular season, averaging 11.7 points per game. (Nhat V. Meyer/Staff)

That his intensity sometimes manifests itself in loud, public exchanges is just fine with his coach.

"You need guys like that. You have to have that edge," Kerr said. "Particularly on our team, we're a pretty quiet group. I love that he's loud."

Green said people connect in different ways, but that he and Kerr understand each other.

"If you look back, he played with that same fire I play with. It's not like we're polar opposites," Green said. "Sometimes it'll clash a little bit. It never clashes out of disrespect. It's more respect than anything.

"We both get each other fired up. I'm mean fired up. It's fun. I don't take it personal when he yells at me and screams and goes crazy, even if it's not my fault. I might get mad, but I don't take it personal. And he don't take it personal when I say something to him."

The passion is a family trait, Green said, and no one exhibits it more than his mother, Mary Babers-Green, especially when she is firing off her in-game thoughts on Twitter. "She is something special," said Green, explaining he was up until 4 in the morning after Game 2 reading all her tweets.

The key to making relationships work, Green said, is to adjust to each person. He felt like he could say anything to former coach Mark Jackson but the tone was different because Jackson is an ordained minister who does not curse.

Without the verbal cuffs, his exchanges with Kerr are more like the relationship he formed with Tom Izzo, his coach at Michigan State.

The details don't matter, Green said.

"We've got one common goal, and that's to win a championship." ∎

Draymond Green defends Cleveland's LeBron James during Game 2 of the NBA Finals. One of the most intense players on the Warriors' roster, Green's defense was a key asset in the Warriors' title run. (Jose Carlos Fajardo/Staff)

SWEET SPLASH

CURRY RECEIVES 100 OF THE 130 FIRST-PLACE VOTES

BY DIAMOND LEUNG • MAY 5, 2015

Stephen Curry, the Warriors' dynamo who was shaped by setbacks and scrawny beginnings, cried when family members surprised him with the news he was voted the NBA's Most Valuable Player.

He took a seat and thought about those who had helped him along the way, shaking his head with the trophy in front of him. Then he delivered an emotional hourlong speech Monday at the Oakland Convention Center, choking up as he celebrated how family in the front row and teammates seated on stage had inspired him.

"This is not possible without you guys," Curry said. "I want everybody to get a fingerprint on that so I can remember who I rolled with during this year, and thank you from the bottom of my heart."

Curry, 27, became the second player in franchise history to win the MVP award, joining Wilt Chamberlain, who won it in 1960 playing for the Philadelphia Warriors.

Curry received 100 of 130 possible first-place votes after leading the Warriors to a league-best 67-15 record. The Houston Rockets' James Harden finished second and earned 25 first-place votes after the MVP for months centered on the two players.

"Everybody was saying that because I had a good team and good teammates that that might hurt my MVP case," Curry said. "If that were the case, then I wouldn't want the award, because it's about winning. It's a team game."

In the end, Curry won in a landslide. He was the only player to appear on every ballot, receiving 26 second-place votes, three third-place votes and a fifth-place vote. The runner-up Harden collected 87 second-place votes.

Curry thanked everyone from coach Steve Kerr's staff to the team's equipment manager and public relations assistants. He failed to hold back tears as he addressed his father, Dell, who played 16 NBA seasons.

"To be able to follow in your footsteps," Curry said, pausing, "it means a lot to me."

Curry acknowledged how having a father in the NBA didn't guarantee him success in basketball. He was the smallest player on his teams growing up and an unranked high school prospect who landed at Davidson College. With the Warriors, he endured ankle injuries and surgeries.

Curry addressed each current teammate individually, shedding light on the relationship he had with each as if reading off a yearbook entry. On the eve of Game 2 of the Western Conference semifinals against Memphis, he said each player was "a reason why this trophy is sitting here, and hopefully another trophy will be sitting here in a few months."

Curry averaged 23.8 points and 7.7 assists per game in the regular season, ranking sixth in both categories while breaking his own single-season record for 3-pointers with 286. He was second to Harden in points scored, led the league shooting 91.4 percent from the free throw line and was fourth with 2.04 steals per game.

A 6-foot-3 point guard, Curry played 32.7 minutes per game for the lowest number out of any player to win the award. But the Warriors in making a case for Curry noted that in his 80 games played, he often sat out entire fourth quarters after having helped the team build large leads. With Curry on the court, the Warriors scored an average of 11.5 more points than they allowed, the highest plus/minus for any player.

NBA Commissioner Adam Silver presents Stephen Curry with the league's Most Valuable Player award before Game 2 of the Western Conference Semifinals against Houston. Curry received 100 of 130 possible first-place votes to become just the second player in Warriors history to earn the award. (Ray Chavez/Staff)

"What makes it so special, there's been other great shooters, but those great shooters didn't have the handle that Steph had," Warriors forward Draymond Green said. "Those great shooters couldn't get in the paint and finish like Steph can. There's been other great ballhandlers. Those great ballhandlers didn't have the shot that he has."

Kerr said he didn't think any player had ever shot the ball as Curry did this season, and it had little to do with his 44.3 shooting percentage from 3-point range.

"Confidence to the point where maybe you dribble behind your back 30 times and take a fadeaway 35-footer and your coach is going, 'Oh my god, what are you doing? Great shot,'" Kerr said.

"And yet the foundation beneath all that is this incredible humility and humanity and a quiet strength. ... Steph is so quiet and humble away from the court, and to me that's the most powerful form of leadership."

Harden was second in the league in scoring at 27.4 points per game, leading the Rockets while perennial All-Star center Dwight Howard missed 41 games mostly because of a knee injury. The shooting guard tied for eighth in the league averaging 7 assists per game.

LeBron James of the Cleveland Cavaliers was third in the voting, the Oklahoma City Thunder's Russell Westbrook was fourth, and the New Orleans Pelicans' Anthony Davis was fifth. Curry's backcourt mate, Klay Thompson, received a fifth-place vote to tie for 10th.

"I think it's well-deserved," James, a four-time winner of the award, told reporters of Curry. "You see first of all the team success. That's the first thing that pops out.

"He's the catalyst of that whole ship, and I think he's had an unbelievable season."

The balloting was conducted through the end of the regular season. Players were awarded 10 points for each first-place vote, seven points for each second-place vote, five for each third-place vote, three for each fourth-place vote and one for each fifth-place vote.

Curry earlier this year also was the leading vote-getter in the All-Star balloting, as he garnered his second straight start in the game and also won the Three-Point Contest.

"I think you all know what he can do on the basketball court, but to be honest, you're missing the best part of all of him if that's all you know," Warriors general manager Bob Myers said. ∎

STEVE KERR

'MY LIFE HAS BEEN SET UP BY CHILDHOOD STABILITY AND INCREDIBLY INTERESTING EXPERIENCES.'

BY JON WILNER • MAY 17, 2015

Steve Kerr played with some of the NBA's greatest players and for several of its greatest coaches. But the man most responsible for Kerr's success as the Warriors' first-year coach was an understated Middle East scholar who enjoyed curing olives and had little interest in professional basketball.

"I'm grateful I had him for 18 years," Kerr said recently in a rare interview about his father. "I feel his full impact on my whole life. It's there every day."

Malcolm Kerr was assassinated in the winter of 1984, gunned down by Islamic terrorists at the American University of Beirut.

His athletic endeavors extended no further than shooting hoops with his kids in the driveway, but the upbringing Malcolm and his wife, Ann, provided would infuse Kerr with a worldly perspective and ability to adapt to anyone and any situation.

Before he learned the game from Hall of Fame coaches such as Phil Jackson, Kerr learned German in a French elementary school.

Before he caught a pass from Michael Jordan and hit the shot to win the NBA title, Kerr attended a backyard barbecue with Egyptian royalty.

Before he set foot in a Warriors locker room that was reeling from the departure of his popular predecessor, Kerr spent years navigating his way around Cairo.

"My life has been set up by childhood stability and incredibly interesting experiences," said Kerr, the third of four children. "That's helped me as a player and a coach. I have a much better understanding of people."

That skill has proved invaluable for the rookie coach of a young team one step from the NBA Finals.

***

There were two bullets.

Fired from silencer-equipped revolvers on the morning of Jan. 18, 1984, they struck Malcolm Kerr in the back of the head in the hallway outside his office. The 52-year-old president of the American University of Beirut, who had accepted his dream job 16 months earlier, crumpled to the floor.

A group calling itself the Islamic Holy War,

Warriors head coach Steve Kerr answers questions from the media on June 2, 2015. In his first season as an NBA head coach, Kerr led the Warriors to a franchise-record 67 wins. (D. Ross Cameron/Staff)

which opposed American presence in Lebanon, claimed responsibility for the assassination, according to the New York Times.

Half a world away, just after midnight, the phone rang in Kerr's freshman dorm room at the University of Arizona. A family friend relayed the unthinkable news. Kerr hung up, then ran into the streets of Tucson.

"I didn't know what else to do," he said.

Separated from family, his world crashing down, Kerr realized there was one thing he could do: Play basketball. So the next day, he practiced. The day after that, he played.

Kerr wept through a moment of silence for his father prior to tipoff against archrival Arizona State. Then he came off the bench and made his first shot. Cheers, tears … bedlam.

He became Tucson's adopted son that day, but the game that defined his college career came four years later and 100 miles up the road in Tempe.

As Kerr warmed up on the court 30 minutes before tipoff, a small group of Arizona State students positioned themselves nearby and began their barbaric chant:

"P.L.O.!"

"P.L.O.!"

"Where's your dad?"

Trembling, Kerr dropped the ball and staggered to the Arizona bench. Tears welled in his eyes.

"I will never, ever forget that," said KNBR host Tom Tolbert, who played with Kerr for two years at Arizona and remains a close friend. "It was the only time I've seen him break down.

"I couldn't believe the words coming out of their mouths. I went to the locker room because if I didn't, I would have gone into the stands."

In the blowout victory that followed, Kerr drained six 3-pointers.

In the first half.

***

The Kerrs arrived in the Middle East in 1919, when Stanley and Elsa — Steve's grandparents — joined relief efforts in the wake of the Armenian genocide. They eventually moved to Beirut and joined the faculty at the American University. Malcolm was born and raised in the Lebanese city, and he

Steve Kerr high-fives the Dub Nation faithful after the Warriors win the Western Conference Finals. [Nhat V. Meyer/Staff]

would meet his future wife at the university.

Ann Zwicker arrived in Beirut in 1954. A student at Occidental College, she crossed the Atlantic in 17 days aboard a Dutch freighter, then settled in for her junior year at the American University. She had four Arab roommates, immersed herself in Ottoman history and, within a month, had met Malcolm.

They were married in Santa Monica in 1956 and began a life together that would crisscross the continents in the name of academia and adventure.

Pacific Palisades became the family's home base after Malcolm joined UCLA's political science department, but they returned frequently to the Middle East. (He would become the leading Western authority on Lebanon.)

Steve Kerr was born in the hospital at the American University and spent his toddler years in Beirut before the family returned to Southern California. They packed up again in the early 1970s — Malcolm was on sabbatical — and set their sights on Tunisia and France. Kerr attended kindergarten in Provence, France.

"The first day I was there, I had to go to the bathroom," he recalled. "I didn't know how to ask in French, so I peed my pants.

"I went to the office, and they put me in checkered slacks."

Not long after, a teacher mentioned to Ann that little "Stephon" was making great progress with his German.

German?

"We thought he was learning French," Ann said. "So he came home and we asked him to count to 10. Sure enough, it was eins, zwei, drei."

The family returned to Los Angeles, and Kerr's passion for sports blossomed. He became a ball boy for the UCLA basketball team and attended Dodgers games, often arriving early enough to chase batting practice home runs. One-on-one basketball in the driveway with his brother John, older by four years, usually ended with Kerr losing the game and his cool, unable to channel his hypercompetitiveness.

"Oh, I had a horrible temper," Kerr said. "If I didn't get a hit, or missed a shot, I'd throw these huge tantrums. But my dad would never grab me right away. He was patient. He'd wait until I calmed down to talk to me.

"My dad taught me a lot about emotions, controlling my temper and being even-keeled."

When he wasn't playing with his four kids, Malcolm

worked. He'd come home and head into his study to read or write. Family dinners often included faculty friends from UCLA or guests from the Middle East.

During a backyard barbecue with Queen Farida of Egypt, Kerr's older sister, Susan, acted on a dare and asked, "Would you like another meatball, your royal highness?"

The lifestyle helped foster curiosity in the Kerr children.

John has a doctorate in applied economics from Stanford and is a professor at Michigan State.

Susan earned her doctorate in education from Harvard and is a politician in England.

Andrew, the youngest, followed Steve at Arizona, worked for the National Security Council, then got his MBA at the Thunderbird School of Global Management and works in the construction business.

"I joke with Steve that he's the dumbest one in the family," said Bruce Fraser, a Warriors player development coach and one of Kerr's closest friends. "He's the least educated but the most wealthy."

Ann's description: "I have two Ph.D.s, one MBA and one NBA."

The family returned to the Middle East in 1977, when Malcolm became a visiting professor at the American University in Cairo. Kerr attended junior high school and one year of high school in the ancient city, learning halting Arabic and forging friendships with kids from all over the world.

He wasn't happy about being removed from the American "basketball track," as Ann described it, but the experience left a lasting impression.

"You have to learn to fit in when you're the outsider, and that gives you more understanding when someone else is the outsider," John said. "Steve is totally comfortable with what he doesn't know."

***

Kerr spoke at length about his childhood during a recent interview and credits both parents, working in concert across continents, to provide "everything I needed." But in personality, Kerr said, he is wired like his father: reserved but passionate (the father about Lebanon, the son about basketball), thoughtful but possessing a razor-sharp wit.

Kerr's memories remain vivid all these years later, and he rattled them off: There is Malcolm, reading the New Yorker in the stands at Dodger Stadium. There is Malcolm, coming

Steve Kerr shows his fiery personality during Game 2 of the Western Conference Finals against Houston. (Dan Honda/Staff)

home from the office and making popcorn. There is Malcolm, emerging from his study to shoot baskets in the driveway.

And there is Malcolm, patiently waiting for his enraged son to settle down.

"He set such a good example," said Kerr, who has three children. "I've tried to be the same way with my kids."

The lessons imparted at home and the experiences gained overseas — "They all got thrown into bathwater and survived," Ann said — combined to shape Kerr's worldview, foster a sense of empathy and sharpen his interpersonal skills.

Those same skills would help carry him through a 15-year NBA career — a second-round draft pick, he won five NBA championships with the Chicago Bulls and San Antonio Spurs — and ease his transition to coaching.

"I developed a lot of compassion living in Egypt, seeing the poverty," he said. "The discussions around the dinner table about world politics and understanding how fortunate we were — all that helped me gain perspective on life.

"That helped with teammates when I was a player and now as a coach."

Early in his acceptance speech for being named the NBA's Most Valuable Player, guard Stephen Curry thanked Kerr for not letting the Warriors get complacent and noted, "You're very humble in the way you've approached this season."

Kerr's first move spoke volumes: He assembled a first-class coaching staff, with lieutenants (Alvin Gentry and Ron Adams) who were better versed than he in critical aspects of the game.

He never felt threatened by the players' fondness for former coach Mark Jackson and allowed them to keep several traditions from the Jackson era.

He gained Curry's trust, inspired disillusioned center Andrew Bogut, managed David Lee's reduced role and convinced veteran Andre Iguodala, a longtime NBA starter, to come off the bench.

"You're a huge reason why we're here today," Curry said as he turned to Kerr during the MVP acceptance speech. "Thanks very much for being you." ∎

40
HARRISON BARNES

GAME PROVIDES 'SENATOR' PLATFORM TO EFFECT CHANGE

BY DANIEL BROWN • MAY 18, 2015

On the day he won the MVP award in a landslide, Stephen Curry was already looking ahead to another election. The Warriors guard used his news conference to launch the political campaign of teammate Harrison Barnes.

"You've got my vote when you run for whatever office," Curry said.

The line got a chuckle. But it wasn't a joke.

Barnes, 22, really does have political aspirations. It's a course he has been plotting since he was a kid in Ames, where he watched presidential hopefuls blaze through town as part of the Iowa caucuses.

"They lit the state on fire," Barnes recalled. "There was so much craziness going on. I kind of got exposed to the landscape like that. It made me aware at a young age that that's how change is supposed to happen."

For now, of course, Barnes has his own craziness going on. The Warriors are in the Western Conference finals for the first time since the Gerald Ford administration. They host the Houston Rockets in Game 1 on Tuesday.

Barnes' approval ratings are way up after a strong performance in the conference semifinals. He scored double-digits in all six games against the Memphis Grizzlies, shooting 54.4 percent.

"Harrison Barnes is quietly having a tremendous series and doesn't get enough credit," Memphis coach Dave Joerger said after Game 5.

The future political candidate apparently believes in a strong defense. Coach Steve Kerr praised the 225-pound Barnes during the series for helping the Warriors control the 260-pound Zach Randolph.

"That's what makes Harrison unique: The fact he's strong enough to guard a guy like Zach Randolph — obviously, with help," Kerr said. "He's strong enough to hold off some of the league's best power forwards for periods of the game. He's quick enough to switch onto a point guard."

When Barnes talks about some of the players he admires most, though, he mentions a different type of versatility. He's a big fan of Bill Bradley, the former New York Knicks small forward better known for his three terms as a U.S. Senator.

Barnes also keeps an eye on Kevin Johnson, the three-time All-Star now serving as the mayor of Sacramento. He said a few weeks ago that he planned to pick Johnson's brain this summer about the transition from hoops to high office.

Harrison Barnes elevates to dunk the ball during the Warriors' series-clinching win over the Houston Rockets in the Western Conference Finals. The third-year forward started all 82 regular season games for the Warriors, averaging 10.1 points and 5.5 rebounds. (Doug Duran/Staff)

"It's something I've thought about," Barnes said after a recent practice. "I don't know if it's holding a position at the state level or at the national level or just going grass-roots style and trying to effect change that way."

Just in case, Barnes carries himself with an air of diplomacy. He's so stately and impressive during interviews that broadcaster Jim Barnett has nicknamed him "The Senator."

It's nothing new. Barnes has been image-conscious since he was a teenager living in the spotlight as the one of the nation's top high school recruits.

"You're definitely much more aware of how you carry yourself," Barnes said. "You understand that you're an example to lots of young kids. So you know that everything you do has an effect.

"On the other hand, it also gives you a platform. You get to voice your opinion. So if you want to have something changed, or bring awareness to something, you have a platform for that as well."

Barnes played at North Carolina, where coach Roy Williams insisted players wear suits in the public eye. Barnes and his teammates did the same thing at Ames High. "They didn't even fit," Barnes said with a laugh. "We just wanted to look the part."

Barnes graduated near the top of his class and helped the team win the Iowa 4A state championship. (He completed nine advance-placement classes before graduating high school.)

He owes his polish to his mother, Shirley, who had a template in mind while raising her children. Shirley idolized Michael Jordan for his talent on the court and for his composure off it. Just to make it clear whom her son should take after, she named him Harrison Bryce Jordan Barnes.

When her children got older, Shirley ran Harrison and his younger sister Jourdan-Ashle through mock news conferences to sharpen their interview skills. An ESPN.com profile of Shirley in 2011 said the exercise was inspired by a church service.

"Our pastor gave a sermon and his message was, 'Don't tell it all,' meaning don't give up more than what people ask," Shirley told ESPN. "Let them see who you are by what you do."

Harrison Barnes' rehearsed image has a flip side, however. He risks coming across as buttoned-up, even aloof. Teammates at North Carolina used to tease him for thinking so much about his brand while still in school. Barnes once had a logo made up — "The Black Falcon," a reference to one of his other nicknames — but that idea never took flight.

Barnes' play can look overly careful, too. The seventh pick of the 2012 draft averaged a pedestrian 9.6 points over his first three seasons. Teammates have encouraged him to bring more of a snarl, which is why teammate Draymond Green praised his play after his 14-performance against the Grizzlies in Game 5.

"When he's aggressive like that, he's tough to stop," Green told reporters. "He's so athletic and fundamentally sound."

Barnes laughs off the notion that he's too serious. He recently hosted a "Game of Thrones" party for some selected Twitter followers and still goes rapturous over his favorite TV show, "Breaking Bad."

And, Barnes noted, he's not always on the campaign trail.

"When you see me on the street, you're not going to see me in a suit and tie," he said. "You're going to see me in sweats, T-shirts and sandals."

Barnes never mentioned a political party during this conversation, but he cited two causes close to his heart. He said he's a big fan of the "Free America" campaign launched by musician John Legend. The goal is to end mass incarceration by changing the penalties for some crimes.

He also likes Michelle Obama's "Let's Move!" initiative to combat obesity.

Barnes' own platform will have to wait.

For one thing, he left UNC after two years and needs go back to finish his major in business administration.

There's also the matter of the Warriors' opportunity to win their first NBA championship since 1975.

Barnes has Curry's endorsement in that regard, too.

"You are wise beyond your years and a huge catalyst for our success the last three years," the MVP said after winning the award. "(You) just getting better every single year has been huge for us." ∎

Harrison Barnes skies to the hoop before being fouled by the Grizzlies' Zach Randolph during Game 5 of the Western Conference Semifinals. (Jane Tyska/Staff)

PERFECTION

KERR PUT TOGETHER PERFECT COACHING STAFF

BY TIM KAWAKAMI • MAY 19, 2015

Sometimes, probably most times, Steve Kerr's Warriors coaching staff looks and acts like a lively bunch of high achieving, highly diverse camp counselors.

That's exactly the way Kerr assembled his group of five formidable assistants, and that was how they were all splayed out on the Warriors' practice court a few weeks ago.

There was veteran Ron Adams twisting on the floor into yoga positions, longtime Kerr pal Bruce Fraser feeding passes to Stephen Curry, and rookie assistants Luke Walton and Jarron Collins yelping and thrashing with a few Warriors bench players in a three-on-three game.

Later, top aide Alvin Gentry wandered out to pore over some video with Festus Ezeli as Kerr started spilling into yoga positions himself.

Before that, Kerr looked around, beamed, and pointed out this was the exact realization of his plan when he built his staff last summer.

"I wanted experience on either side of me," Kerr said, referring to Gentry and Adams, before gesturing to the three-on-three game.

"And then I wanted this, right here, what you're seeing. I wanted guys like Luke or Jarron who had just finished playing, who could get out on the floor and be more physical with the players ...

"For them to be able to go to one of our players and say, 'When I guarded Dwight Howard, this is how I approached it.' You need some hands-on experience from guys who have actually done it."

Well, it turns out the Warriors are actually playing Dwight Howard and Houston now in the Western Conference finals, starting with Game 1 on Tuesday, after the Warriors' slugfest six-game victory over Memphis.

Which leads us to the other manifestation of Kerr's staff — something that can only happen organically, and under extreme pressure.

Down 2-1 against the Grizzlies, with Game 4 coming up in Memphis, Kerr's staff hunkered down in a hotel meeting room and evolved into something close to an adrenaline-fueled team of brilliant attorneys brainstorming before the biggest day of a murder trial.

That was Kerr's plan, too, from the outset — everybody from the video assistants to Kerr to the players has had a voice this entire season.

"Steve is one of those guys — he's secure in his own skin," Adams said. "He's a bright guy; he's had a wealth of basketball experience. OK, so he's learning the coaching thing this year and I would say he's learned it at a high rate and very well.

"He's a really good leader of our team. But he wants input."

In the Memphis series, there was one key strategic moment, when the Warriors decided in Game 4 to switch center Andrew Bogut onto Memphis guard Tony Allen and skinny small forward Harrison Barnes onto

Golden State Warriors head coach Steve Kerr shares a laugh with veteran assistant Alvin Gentry during a victory against the Brooklyn Nets in November. (Jose Carlos Fajardo/Staff)

burly Grizzlies power forward Zach Randolph.

It helped turn the series and the Warriors swept the final three games.

"That was Ron," Collins said, appreciatively. "Ron actually mentioned that on the plane going down to Memphis (before Game 3), as an idea, putting Bogues on Tony Allen.

"Obviously we didn't do it until Game 4, but as soon as he mentioned it, I thought it was fascinating, because I was trying to think in my mind offensively how would they combat that and it was no easy answer."

Clearly, Adams on the defensive side and Gentry on the offensive side are the two staff stalwarts — and they are two of the highest-paid assistants in the league.

"Alvin sees it from an offensive perspective; Ron sees everything from a defensive perspective," Kerr said. "I believe Ron would like to win a game 4-2. And I don't think Alvin would mind winning 138-130."

The sessions are spirited, especially when the season is on the line.

But all of the principals say there are no major disagreements, just debate and questions and more debate.

As Collins said, if you have a point, you have to be able to defend it.

"I think Alvin is key to this," Adams said. "Alvin has a great wealth of experience, really a fine offensive coach.

"But he's always very respectful of Steve and Steve's ideas. I think that has really made that work."

Even before he was officially hired by the Warriors a year ago, Kerr was thinking about the proper mix and meshing of personalities.

The calm, sardonic Gentry was the coach in Phoenix when Kerr was the general manager; Collins was a player there; Kerr knows Walton from their twin Arizona backgrounds; Kerr knew many basketball people who swore by the professorial, demanding Adams.

"I wanted to be around people who I enjoyed every day," Kerr said. "These guys are all fantastic; they all have a different life perspective, different background. They all are fun to be around and very funny."

Beyond Gentry, who, as a former NBA head coach (and a leading candidate to get another top job this summer),

serves as Kerr's main sounding board, and Adams, the others have carved out roles.

Walton tends to be involved more on the offensive side and is in the timeout huddles with Kerr and Gentry before Kerr speaks to the team.

Walton and Adams also have developed a wry byplay, mostly as seatmates on long plane rides.

"Luke, he's my German Shepherd puppy," Adams said. "He and I just hit it off really well. He knows I'm kind of nutty and he's kind of nutty."

Collins is the studious Stanford product who happens to have drawn the main scouting responsibilities for New Orleans in the first round and now Houston. (Walton had the scout for Memphis last round.)

"He hasn't been removed from playing that many years," Gentry said of Collins. "I kid him about that Stanford education, that elitist education they've had. (Smiles.)

"But the players really respect him because he's really conscientious; he's going to do a scouting report, he goes beyond the call of duty, which tells me he's really dedicated."

Fraser, one of Kerr's best friends, works with Curry and Klay Thompson, among others, and acts as an emotional barometer for the team.

"I think I may be more on the philosophical side, how our guys are feeling, what the message of the team is, what the mood, what the other team did to us," Fraser said.

The Warriors players — after some bumpy times with Mark Jackson's staff last season — have embraced the new level of cohesion.

The 67-victory regular season, the MVP for Stephen Curry, and the journey through two rounds of the playoffs ... well, that helps solidify everything.

"I feel like they really studied each guy's personality when they brought them in," Bogut said. "Because they're all great guys, first and foremost, but they're also a little bit different.

"You never want to have a coaching staff that's all trying to be like each other, you know what I mean? It becomes like a PTA meeting at a high school."

No, the Warriors staff isn't a PTA meeting. It's competitive, it's a group of jokesters, and it's a crackling strategic hothouse, all in one, all at once, all just the way Kerr hoped and planned. ■

Steve Kerr goes over strategy with his players during an April 2015 game at Oracle Arena. The Warriors rookie head coach credits his five assistant coaches for playing a critical role in the team's success. (Ray Chavez/Staff)

12
ANDREW BOGUT

ONCE AN ACCLAIMED PLAYMAKER, BOGUT NOW EXCELS AS A GRITTY DEFENDER

BY DANIEL BROWN • JUNE 3, 2015

Andrew Bogut's favorite player growing up was hardly an enforcer. Bogut loved Toni Kukoc, the spindly-limbed "Croatian Sensation" known for his flashy play with the Chicago Bulls of the mid-1990s.

"I had a very similar body to him as a young fellow," the Warriors center said Monday, recalling the days when he was a mere 6-foot-8 and 190 pounds. "I was really lanky. I saw this guy playing for the Bulls that had the same body as me and he was doing all of these special things."

Bogut emulated Kukoc's style and grew up to be a 7-footer with a stylish small forward's game.

His ability to run, pass, handle the ball and shoot with either hand made him the No. 1 pick in the NBA draft in 2005.

Now, his willingness to abandon all that offensive flair has the Warriors on the brink of an NBA title.

Bogut has made it to the place No. 1 picks are supposed to reach, though not in the way college scouts once imagined. He long ago gave up a starring role to take a job as a bouncer.

The 260-pound Australian is the Warriors' snarling presence on defense, the guy willing to trade elbows with Dwight Howard, bang bodies with Zach Randolph and take verbal jabs at Mark Jackson.

You've heard Stephen Curry described as the "Baby-Faced Assassin?"

Bogut is the Assassin-Faced Assassin.

"When he's on the floor for us, he changes the game at (the defensive) end," Curry said after practice this week. "He erases a lot of mistakes. ... He can impact shots whether he's blocking them or not."

All eyes will be on Curry and LeBron James when the Warriors and Cleveland Cavaliers open the NBA Finals on Thursday at Oracle Arena. But the worthy undercard includes Bogut squaring off against Timofey Mozgov, the Cavs' 7-foot-1, 250-pounder who is averaging 9.1 points and 7.2 rebounds in the playoffs.

Their last showdown was a decisive victory for Mozgov. He outplayed Bogut offensively and defensively during Cleveland's 110-99 home victory Feb. 26.

Bogut will have to do better, and his teammates suspect he will.

"Steph makes our offense go," forward Draymond Green said. "Bogut makes our defense go."

Bogut is coming off a regular season in which he posted a career-low 23.6 minutes, and his 6.3 scoring average was his lowest in a full season. His deft interior passing is the last vestige of his days as an offensive threat.

He also has never been more important. When Bogut was in the starting lineup this season with Curry, Klay Thompson, Harrison Barnes and Green, the Warriors went 50-7.

The second-team selection on the NBA All-Defensive Team sets screens, grabs rebounds and scraps to make sure Curry and Thompson can spring free for feet-set three-pointers. Bogut finished second in the

NBA in defensive rating, trailing only Kawhi Leonard of the San Antonio Spurs.

The advanced stat known as Defensive Box Plus/Minus rated Bogut tops in the league, just ahead of Utah's Rudy Gobert.

Defensive 'Anchor'

Bogut, who still sees the court like a point guard, barks out assignments to his fellow defenders when he's on the court.

"He's the anchor of our defense. He's the back line. He's the voice," Green said. "He's not afraid to tell you, 'Hey, you should be doing this instead of that.'"

Festus Ezeli said: "He's the 'eraser' for us. I learned a lot from him defensively, just in terms of positioning, demeanor, professionalism. Everything. He's somebody that doesn't get a lot of credit for what he does."

Bogut's greatest contribution this season? Remaining upright. He played 65 of 82 regular-season games, missing a handful here and there mostly for bone edema chondromalacia.

Edema can be extremely painful, but it was nothing compared to a pair of horrific injuries that threatened his career.

"My body still feels great," Bogut said after practice Monday. "There are still days when I'm really sore, but for the most part I feel pretty good, and I've played 80-odd games this season (including the postseason).

"Hopefully, it can be four more wins and a beautiful offseason."

Bogut was finishing up a breakout season with the Milwaukee Bucks on April 3, 2010, when things went horribly awry. He soared up for a dunk but tumbled over Amare Stoudemire of the Phoenix Suns and fell, as NBA.com writer Ian Thomsen recently recounted, "as if from a second-story window. His right arm was extended beneath him gruesomely as he landed."

Bogut said he sustained a dislocated arm, a broken bone in his elbow and broke both sides of his wrist. He also broke two fingers and suffers enduring trauma to his right shooting arm.

"Sometimes I will shoot and my elbow will give out and it will hurt, like a stabbing pain," Bogut told NBA.com. "And then the next time when I shoot it's fine. And I don't know when it's going to come."

Bogut later suffered another epic setback, a fractured ankle on Jan. 25, 2012. That eventually led to microfracture surgery — and another trouble-plagued comeback trail.

You want to risk your own health? Ask Bogut about being "injury prone." It's a label he flatly rejects, reasoning that this isn't exactly a tweaked hamstring here or a stiff shoulder there.

Bogut describes his injuries as "catastrophic." So his disdain was palpable on the night Jackson, his coach a year ago, suggested to reporters that Bogut may have injured a shoulder just lying around. "It may have been sleeping, and I say that in all seriousness," Jackson said then.

Bogut, given a chance to respond, snapped: "That sleeping comment is absolutely ridiculous," setting off a simmering feud with Jackson that has yet to abate. Jackson will be on hand for the series as an ABC analyst.

Health at Forefront

These days, the Warriors manage Bogut's minutes with an eye toward the long haul. In a way, it's the same thing the Giants have done with Buster Posey ever since the All-Star catcher returned from a horrific ankle injury.

The Warriors look for creative ways to manage Bogut's playing time, knowing they're unlikely to win a championship without him. He topped 30 minutes of playing time in a game only five times over his final 47 regular-season games.

This might not be the career trajectory fans envisioned when Bogut came out of Utah, back when his smooth offensive game drew comparisons to Vlade Divac, Bill Walton and a young Arvydas Sabonis.

Before the NBA draft that year, New Mexico coach Ritchie McKay told Sports Illustrated, "Bogut is an impossible matchup. He's the best big-man passer I've ever seen in college. He makes everyone on his team better, and that's rare for a post player."

Now, he's a grunt. And Bogut loves it. In contrast to his clashes with Jackson, Bogut has embraced new coach Steve Kerr's defensive-minded mentality and insistence on fundamentals.

Someone asked Bogut on Monday what advice he would give to young players who have NBA dreams.

The center's answer no longer had anything to do with a highlight reel.

"Put in the work," Bogut said. "Instead of tweeting or Instagram-ing, 'Grind hard,' 'Work hard' and all that crap, go out and do it. That's not just in sports. In anything in life: You have a chance to make something of yourself." ∎

GAME 1

APRIL 18, 2015 • OAKLAND, CALIFORNIA
WARRIORS 106, PELICANS 99

FLEXING OUT OF THE GATE

AFTER DOMINATING FOR THREE QUARTERS, WARRIORS BARELY HOLD ON

BY DIAMOND LEUNG

The Warriors began their playoff run with a win that was a bit too close for comfort for the team that finished the regular season with the best record in the NBA.

The 106-99 Game 1 victory Saturday didn't come easily for the Warriors, even after dominating New Orleans for most of the game at Oracle Arena.

"Not great," Warriors center Andrew Bogut said of the mood in the locker room. "We didn't finish the game off right."

Said forward Draymond Green of the win: "C-plus, B-minus because there are a lot of things we can do better."

But despite high expectations, the Warriors will certainly take a win in which Stephen Curry scored 34 points and they led by as many as 25 points in the third quarter.

"Look, for the most part, we played a really good game," coach Steve Kerr said. "If you go into the fourth quarter up 18, you've done a pretty good job."

They then had to survive New Orleans' furious comeback attempts, as the Pelicans battled back behind star forward Anthony Davis' 35 points and cut the lead to 103-99 with 9.7 seconds left.

The Warriors saw eight of their 13 missed free throws come in the fourth quarter, doing just enough to hang on to the win.

When the Pelicans responded with a 14-0 run, Curry and Klay Thompson buried back-to-back 3-pointers to push the Warriors' fourth-quarter lead back to 17.

When New Orleans cut the lead to eight with less than two minutes remaining, Green scored and proceeded to twice direct flexing at Davis.

Green racked up 15 points, 12 rebounds and seven assists while doing yeoman's work guarding Davis.

In his postseason debut against the more experienced Warriors, Davis still scored 24 points in the second half and grabbed seven rebounds while committing five turnovers.

"We're going to fight to the end," Davis said. "We showed that today.

"We just got to continue to fight and make adjustments."

Bogut, back in the playoffs after sitting out last year's festivities because of injury, helped bother Davis and also collected 12 points on 6-for-8 shooting along with 14 rebounds. Thompson added 21 points.

The Warriors were dominant at the start, taking a 28-13 lead after the first quarter. It was the fewest points they had allowed in the first quarter of a playoff game in franchise history.

Curry scored 11 points in the first, including a deep 3-pointer over Davis that capped a 10-0 run that

Draymond Green celebrates his strong play — 15 points, 12 rebounds, seven assists and solid defense on Anthony Davis — during Game 1 of the series. (Jose Carlos Fajardo/Staff)

grabbed the lead from the Pelicans for good.

Thompson completed a 3-point play and nailed a shot from beyond the arc in response to the Pelicans scoring eight straight points to start the second.

Curry finished in transition with a reverse layup high off the glass as Davis fouled him, and the three-point play gave the Warriors a 59-41 halftime lead as they went into the locker room riding a 15-2 run.

"When you compare it to the end of the game and how close we got it, it makes you think about the start," Pelicans coach Monty Williams said, adding that it was human nature for his players making their first postseason appearances to have to settle down from some anxiety at halftime.

It didn't help New Orleans that point guard Tyreke Evans left the game in the second quarter because of a left knee contusion. He was scheduled to undergo an MRI exam.

Still, the Pelicans outscored the Warriors 33-22 in the fourth quarter with Norris Cole and Quincy Pondexter facilitating shots for Davis. Pondexter guarded Curry and held him to 4-for-13 shooting from 3-point range while finishing with 20 points, nine rebounds and six assists.

The last laugh went to Curry, who said there would be no panic coming from the Warriors despite a lackluster finish.

"They're obviously a talented team that's going to make a couple runs here and there, but nothing is going to be easy this series," Curry said.

"Just find a way to get a win. That's the key as you go through the playoffs. No matter how pretty it is or ugly it is, a win is a win." ■

GAME 2

APRIL 20, 2015 • OAKLAND, CALIFORNIA

WARRIORS 97, PELICANS 87

RAUCOUS AND VICTORIOUS

WARRIORS REPEL PELICANS' CHALLENGE, TAKE 2-0 SERIES LEAD

BY DIAMOND LEUNG

The Warriors heard New Orleans challenge their home-court advantage with pregame comments and then were tested by the Pelicans' willingness to hang in a hostile environment.

Undeterred, the Warriors stood tall in the face of an upset bid and clawed out a 97-87 win against the Pelicans at Oracle Arena on Monday to take a 2-0 lead in the first-round playoff series.

Klay Thompson scored 18 of his 26 points in the second half, and Stephen Curry added 22 points to lead the top-seeded Warriors, who also got key contributions from their celebrated second unit.

Draymond Green, playing on a left ankle he twice tweaked in the game, had 14 points, 12 rebounds and five assists while getting key stops on defense.

Pelicans star Anthony Davis scored 26 points but was 0 for 5 from the field in the fourth quarter while being held to six free throws.

"It's a lot to ask, but we feel like the identity of our team is our defense and our versatility at that end," Warriors coach Steve Kerr said. "I thought Draymond was just fantastic. (Andrew) Bogut fantastic, and the defense carried the day."

Before the game at the Pelicans' shootaround, coach Monty Williams raised some eyebrows with comments questioning whether or not the noise level at Oracle Arena was legal and complained that it "does get a little out of hand."

Williams said he meant it as a compliment. The crowd didn't take it that way, roaring so loudly during the Pelicans' pregame introductions that the public address announcer could hardly be heard.

"Monty should have never said that, so we knew the (fans) were going to come in with a lot of energy," the Warriors' Marreese Speights said.

They had plenty to cheer about late in the game, as while Davis kept missing, the Warriors went on a 10-0 run to finish off the Pelicans.

"Down the stretch, there were times where we tried to push it, and we got a stop and we turned it over, then they rammed it right back down our throat," Williams said.

Eric Gordon added 23 points for New Orleans, which led at one point by 13 points. But in the end, the Warriors were too much at home, where they were 39-2 in the regular season.

Leandro Barbosa added 12 points off the bench, and Speights had five points and two blocks to get the Warriors going on a night when they shot only 44.2 percent from the field.

"It's win or go home," Curry said. "So the grind-it-out kind of feel of these games here, you expect it's going to be the exact same thing if not tougher in New Orleans."

Klay Thompson elevates during the fourth quarter for two of his game-high 26 points.
(Jose Carlos Fajardo/Staff)

The Warriors despite the raucous crowd came out and struggled in the first quarter, falling behind 28-17.

Cold shooting combined with six early turnovers plagued the Warriors, who shot 31.8 percent from the field in the quarter, including 3 for 10 from 3-point range. Meanwhile, Gordon drained each of his three attempts from long distance and kept momentarily silencing the arena.

It was the bench that brought the Warriors life. The second unit along with Green on the court scored on five of its first six possessions in the second quarter.

Speights buried two jump shots and then assisted on Andre Iguodala's 3-pointer that capped an 11-4 run to cut the deficit to 32-28. Speights' instant offense came after he had played in only 41 seconds of the Warriors' Game 1 win, with the ability to stay ready despite sporadic playing time endearing him to Kerr all season long.

Barbosa also provided a spark with his driving layup and 3-point play, as he became the first Warriors player of the evening to reach the double-digit scoring mark.

The Pelicans held the Warriors at bay with backup point guard Norris Cole catching fire and scoring New Orleans' first nine points of the quarter. The strong guard play was needed with the Pelicans missing Jrue Holiday, who was unable to play because of lower right leg soreness stemming from months of recovery from a stress reaction.

However, Thompson after scuffling in Game 1 got going with back-to-back 3-pointers to tie the score at 47.

Curry's third 3-pointer came on the Warriors' final possession of the half, giving them a 55-52 lead headed into the locker room. He came off the floor clapping with 16 points, knowing that even after the Pelicans had thrown the first punch, the crowd was roaring again. ∎

GAME 3
APRIL 23, 2015 • NEW ORLEANS, LOUISIANA
WARRIORS 123, PELICANS 119, OT

BELIEVE IT!

CURRY, WARRIORS SHOCK PELICANS WITH FURIOUS LATE RALLY

BY DIAMOND LEUNG

Stephen Curry tossed up a rainbow 3-pointer from the corner that tied the score and also served to drive a stake right into the heart of the New Orleans Pelicans.

Curry's shot while falling out of bounds sent the game into an overtime period the Pelicans could have never imagined. The Warriors erased a 20-point deficit in the fourth quarter, as Curry brought them back from the dead for a stunning 123-119 playoff win at New Orleans on Thursday.

The Warriors won a franchise-record 67 games in the regular season, including a league-leading 28 on the road. But none compares to the one they notched against the Pelicans in Game 3 of their first-round series that the Warriors now lead 3-0.

After dominating for most of the game, the Pelicans left a crack open when Anthony Davis missed a free throw with 9.6 seconds left, giving the Warriors a chance to tie it with a 3-pointer.

Of course the ball went to Curry, and the NBA's all-time single-season record-holder in such shots missed his first try. Given a second attempt off a Marreese Speights offensive rebound, Curry threw up some magic from the corner as Davis collided into him. Curry pumped his fists after Tyreke Evans' 3-point attempt at the buzzer missed.

"You give him two looks at that basket? In the corner?" Warriors forward Draymond Green said incredulously. "Oh man, I knew that was money when it left his hand."

Curry scored a game-high 40 points on a night when he wasn't particularly sharp, shooting 10 for 29 from the field. In overtime, he started with his seventh 3-pointer of the game. He finished off the Pelicans with two free throws to give the Warriors a four-point lead with 3.2 seconds left.

The shot from the corner to send the game to overtime was striking.

"To make that shot shows everything that Steph is about," Warriors coach Steve Kerr said. "On a night when he's not even having a great shooting performance, his confidence level is just off the charts. He's fearless."

The Warriors became the third NBA team in the shot-clock era to overcome a 20-point deficit entering the fourth quarter in a playoff game, going on a 20-5 run in the final 4:53 of regulation.

Harrison Barnes cut the deficit to eight points by throwing down a thunderous putback dunk with 3:35 left. A Shaun Livingston tip-in followed by a Green offensive rebound and putback made it 105-101 with 1:40 left.

Livingston drew a foul going for an offensive rebound and hit a free throw with 21.3 seconds left. Curry hit his fifth 3-pointer of the game with 11.8 seconds to cut the lead to two before his dagger to tie the score at 108.

"It's a long game," Curry said of the comeback. "We just stick with it, and it's a sweet feeling to get this win after how the whole game went."

Part of a late comeback, Stephen Curry's buzzer-beating 3-pointer over Anthony Davis sends Game 3 into overtime. (AP Images)

The Warriors grabbed 22 offensive rebounds, including the one Speights grabbed and dished off to Curry that he said was the biggest he's had in his life.

Klay Thompson added 28 points, including six 3-pointers of his own. Green added 12 points, 17 rebounds and five assists.

Davis poured in 29 points, and Ryan Anderson added 26 off the bench, but it wasn't enough. The Warriors can sweep the series with another win in New Orleans on Saturday.

"You can't sugarcoat it," Pelicans coach Monty Williams said. "We're all feeling like dirt right now, so obviously you want to build them up, but there is nothing that can build you up in a situation like that."

The Warriors tried to rally back in the second half after Curry cut the deficit to nine by hitting three straight free throws, including one on a technical. They were met by Davis responding with two straight jump shots to start a 10-0 run

that gave the Pelicans a 19-point lead.

Thompson scored on a 3-point play, and Curry then hit back-to-back 3-pointers, but the Pelicans on Dante Cunningham's dunk pushed the lead to 89-69 at the end of the third.

The Warriors shot 40.4 percent from the field but actually began the game red-hot, with Curry and Thompson combining to hit their first five attempts from 3-point range. The show of firepower left the Warriors with a 17-9 lead, though it did not overwhelm the Pelicans.

Davis had a putback dunk, Evans had a breakaway dunk off a Leandro Barbosa turnover, and Jrue Holiday came off the bench to hit a jump shot to put the Pelicans ahead 26-25 at the end of the first. ■

GAME 4
APRIL 25, 2015 • NEW ORLEANS, LOUISIANA
WARRIORS 109, PELICANS 98

FIRST-ROUND SWEEP

GREEN SCORES 20 IN FIRST QUARTER AS WARRIORS FINISH OFF PELICANS

BY DIAMOND LEUNG

The businesslike Warriors sweeping the New Orleans Pelicans wasn't cause for a large celebration.

Leaving nothing to chance, the Warriors beat the Pelicans 109-98 in Game 4 on Saturday to win the first-round playoff series. Then, the favorites merely flashed some smiles.

"We didn't want to come back here, so the big dogs showed up," the Warriors' Marreese Speights said.

Stephen Curry had 39 points, nine assists and eight rebounds as the top-seeded Warriors advanced to the Western Conference semifinals, where they will face the winner of the Portland-Memphis first-round series that the Grizzlies lead 3-0.

The Warriors led by as many as 24 points and headed into the fourth quarter leading 88-67. After the desperate Pelicans scored nine straight points to start the quarter and an Eric Gordon 3-pointer cut the lead to 95-85 with six minutes left, there was some drama.

The Warriors managed to avoid the fate the Pelicans suffered in Game 3, when they blew a 20-point fourth-quarter lead and lost in overtime. Dante Cunningham's putback dunk made it a seven-point game with 1:16 left, but Klay Thompson responded on the other end with a 3-pointer to seal the series victory.

"Any time you can come into a series against a talented team like they have and you win four straight, that's tough to do against anybody," Curry said. "So I'm proud of the way we played, the way we competed, and

4-0 is a good feeling."

Thompson finished with 25 points, and Draymond Green added 22 points, 10 rebounds and eight assists. Green became the first player with four straight playoff point-rebound double doubles with at least five assists since Tim Duncan in 2003.

Anthony Davis led the Pelicans with 36 points and 11 rebounds, as Warriors coach Steve Kerr said the 22-year-old was "brilliant" and a future MVP.

"I'm very pleased that I don't have to see Anthony Davis until November at the earliest," Kerr said.

According to Curry, Kerr addressed after the morning shoot-around his belief that the team wasn't feeling a sense of urgency after winning the first three games, including an emotional Game 3.

Green then scored 20 points in the first quarter for the most he ever had in a first half of an NBA game. Curry poured in 20 of his own by halftime, as the Warriors went into the locker room in control with a 67-54 lead.

"It's always good for somebody else instead of Steph and Klay to start off hot," Speights said of Green. "He did that and took us home with it."

Golden State was 13 for 24 from 3-point range, including six of those makes coming from Curry.

"There's nothing you can do," Davis said of Curry after the two embraced following the game. "When you try to pressure him and run him off the (3-point) line, he hit incredible shots in the lane. You back off so he won't

Stephen Curry, who had a game-high 39 points, goes to the hoop against Anthony Davis. (AP Images)

drive, he's going to hit a three. You've got to pick your poison."

Davis had led his team to a No. 8 seed in the playoffs to earn MVP consideration, but he indicated that he felt the award was expected to go to either Curry or Houston's James Harden.

"Both of those guys are unbelievable, doing great for their teams," Davis said. "It's going to be exciting to see who wins it. There's no surprise if either guy wins it."

A Curry 3-pointer followed by Green's third of the first quarter gave the Warriors a 31-24 lead, as the two players combined for 27 of those points. Green made his first four shots, scoring 10 of the Warriors' first 13 points.

Curry finished 11 for 20 from the field, including 6 for 8 from 3-point range.

"Hats off to him," Davis said. "They made incredible shots throughout the course of this series."

Curry in turn praised Davis, calling him "a bad boy."

But the series turned out to be all Warriors, who had already done their whooping and hollering after an improbable Game 3 comeback. They earned more opportunities to show their playoff mettle.

"We still feel like we can play better and more consistent," Curry said. ■

GAME 1
MAY 3, 2015 • OAKLAND, CALIFORNIA
WARRIORS 101, GRIZZLIES 86

NO SIGN OF RUST

GOLDEN STATE STORMS PAST MEMPHIS TO OPEN SEMIS

BY DIAMOND LEUNG

The Warriors had their way with Memphis in a 101-86 win in Game 1 of the Western Conference semifinals.

Never mind that the big-bodied Grizzlies can be a load to deal with, as the Warriors shot right past them Sunday to remain undefeated in the postseason.

"You're probably not going to just dominate them inside," Warriors forward Draymond Green said. "That's one of our strengths being able to space them out, so we have to use our strengths against them."

Eight days after playing in their last game, the Warriors showed little signs of rust in executing that game plan.

Stephen Curry scored 22 points, Klay Thompson added 18 and Green had 16, including four 3-pointers.

Memphis' Marc Gasol notched a team-high 21 points along with nine rebounds, while Zach Randolph had 20 points and nine rebounds. But the No. 5-seeded Grizzlies didn't have nearly enough at Oracle Arena to match the Warriors' firepower, as Golden State shot 50.6 percent from the field.

"I didn't feel like the game was physical," Gasol said. "I would tell you if it was, in all honesty. We didn't bring it to that point yet."

Green hit three 3-pointers as the Warriors got off to a hot start. With the Grizzlies missing injured point guard Mike Conley, Curry took advantage of his mismatch with five of his seven assists in the quarter against starter Nick Calathes.

A couple first-quarter developments did give the Warriors cause for concern. Green picked up two fouls. Also, center Andrew Bogut got banged up and limped off the court.

But while playing power forward, Harrison Barnes hung in there with the Grizzlies' big men. His 3-pointer with 7:40 left in the first half gave the Warriors a 45-31 lead.

Marreese Speights also provided a lift off the bench, scoring two baskets in a row to give the Warriors a 16-point advantage. He finished with 10 points, and Festus Ezeli also provided key minutes while Bogut was off the floor.

"We have a lot of depth, and in this series in particular, we're probably going to have to use it because those guys draw a lot of fouls down there," Warriors coach Steve Kerr said, adding that it was a luxury to have Ezeli against Memphis.

Curry's first 3-pointers of the game came on back-to-back possessions in response to the Grizzlies having cut the lead to six points.

"I think we played extremely aggressive, extremely hard in the first half, and take that right where we left off," Curry said.

A deft ballhandler who had seven assists in the game, point guard Stephen Curry dribbles during the first quarter of Game 1. (Nhat V. Meyer/Staff)

The Warriors led 61-52 at halftime and then went on an 11-4 run to start the second half.

"It's always fun, and it's like it's your chance to show your toughness, and you can bang a little bit without getting fouls," Green said of going up against Memphis' front line.

Bogut and Green checked out in the middle of the third with four fouls apiece, but Thompson and Curry extended to the lead to 80-60 after hitting consecutive 3-pointers. Curry's step-back shot from long distance had both Randolph and Beno Udrih going the wrong way trying to defend against it.

Udrih got minutes at point guard and scored seven points, while Calathes went scoreless in 21 minutes.

Conley missed a third straight game but did participate in pregame warm-ups wearing a mask over his face, which sustained fractures in Game 3 of the Grizzlies' first-round playoff series against Portland.

"If we continue to do what we do … on our defensive end, I think we'll be fine regardless of who suits up for them and have that confidence whenever he does come back," Curry said of Conley.

Tony Allen, one of the Grizzlies' top defenders, also got a shot at defending Curry, but the Warriors couldn't be stopped.

Said Curry: "It doesn't matter who's guarding me in that sense, because we're going to do what we do." ■

Above: Raucous Dub Nation fans cheer on their Warriors during Game 1. (Nhat V. Meyer/Staff) Opposite: No shot is too tough for Stephen Curry, who shoots over Vince Carter (15), Jeff Green (32) and Tony Allen (9) of the Grizzlies. (Susan Tripp Pollard/Staff)

GAME 2
MAY 5, 2015 • OAKLAND, CALIFORNIA
GRIZZLIES 97, WARRIORS 90

BIG LETDOWN
INSPIRED GRIZZLIES END WARRIORS' 21-GAME HOME WIN STREAK
BY DIAMOND LEUNG

On Stephen Curry Night at Oracle Arena, the Memphis Grizzlies crashed and shut down the party.

The Grizzlies stunned the Warriors with a 97-90 win Tuesday that evened up the Western Conference semifinals 1-1 as the series heads to Memphis.

After Curry was presented with his MVP trophy before the game by NBA commissioner Adam Silver and declared to the roaring crowd that there was business to take care of, it was the Grizzlies who controlled the tempo the rest of the way.

"It was weird," Curry said of the day's events. "That's the best way I can put it."

The Warriors not only suffered their first loss of the postseason, but saw their 21-game home winning streak stopped cold. It was their first loss of the season when holding their opponent to under 100 points after winning the first 44 of those games.

Curry scored 19 points, but his big day became a mess as the Warriors committed 20 turnovers and shot 41.9 percent from the field and 23.1 percent from 3-point range.

According to coach Steve Kerr, it wasn't so much the Curry festivities that affected the Warriors but rather poise that they lost.

The first Warriors MVP in 55 years was in fact upstaged by gritty Memphis point guard Mike Conley, who made his return from facial surgery and scored a game-high 22 points. Zach Randolph added 20.

Draymond Green had 14 points and 12 rebounds, but shot 3 for 11 from the field. Klay Thompson was held to 13 points on 6-for-15 shooting.

"We weren't going to win every game," Green said. "It's not like this is a walk in the park."

The tone of the game changed early as Green was called for two fouls in the first four minutes and had to take a seat on the bench after being whistled for a technical foul. Replacing him was David Lee, who was still a bit rusty, and the Warriors later turned to Harrison Barnes to play power forward.

The Grizzlies enjoyed having Green off the floor, as Randolph combined with Conley to score 19 of Memphis' first 22 points.

Conley made his first four field goal attempts, scoring nine points in his first quarter of action in 10 days.

With his face still seemingly swollen and his left eye reddened, Conley played in a mask eight days after undergoing facial surgery. He missed three playoff games after taking an elbow to the face in Game 3 of the Grizzlies' first-round series against Portland.

Conley's return to the lineup provided the spark that helped Memphis lead by as many as 11 in the first quarter, finishing it leading 28-22.

In the second quarter as the Warriors cut into the lead, a loose ball with Conley right in the middle of it led to some tempers flaring between the two teams.

With Conley lying on the court with the ball in play, Green reached down to grab it from him and in doing

Stephen Curry tries to get a shot off as the Grizzlies' Tony Allen defends during the fourth quarter of Game 2. Memphis limited Golden State to just 41.9 percent shooting from the field as the Warriors' home winning streak was snapped at 21 games. (Nhat V. Meyer/Staff)

so made contact in the head area. Green was confronted by the Grizzlies' bench as he backed away as if to explain it was accidental contact.

Officials reviewed a potential hostile action by Green on Conley, but no foul was assessed. Green and fellow former Michigan State player Randolph shook hands on the court shortly afterward. Conley was down on the floor momentarily and took his mask off but did not leave the game.

In the meantime, it was the Grizzlies who seized control of the game, closing the half on a 9-0 run to go into the locker room leading 50-39. They became the rare team to hold the Warriors under 40 points in the first half. Only San Antonio had previously achieved that feat this season against Golden State.

"It's not our pace," Green said. "It's more their type of game. It's more their type of game, and they won."

The Grizzlies went on another run to push the lead to

as many as 16 points. Golden State went into the fourth quarter trailing 73-63.

As Conley and Tony Allen clamped down on defense, Curry and Thompson combined for 3-for-13 shooting from beyond the arc after three quarters.

Leandro Barbosa cut the deficit to eight points with back-to-back baskets to start the fourth and Curry and Thompson on the bench.

When Thompson checked back in after a frustrating game, his layup cut the deficit to 81-74. But the Warriors couldn't get stops. Allen picked off a Curry pass and went in for an uncontested dunk to push the lead back up to 11 with 5:34 left.

When the Warriors got the lead back down to seven, Conley again came through with the back-breaking 3-pointer with 2:13 left.

"I thought Mike Conley had tremendous heart," Grizzlies coach Dave Joerger said. ∎

GAME 3
MAY 9, 2015 • MEMPHIS, TENNESSEE
GRIZZLIES 99, WARRIORS 89

GROUND DOWN

WARRIORS WOBBLE IN GRINDHOUSE, FACE 2-1 DEFICIT

BY DIAMOND LEUNG

This time, the Warriors couldn't complete the fourth-quarter comeback.

The Warriors staggered in their slow start and couldn't recover in time as Memphis took a 2-1 lead in Western Conference semifinals with a 99-89 win in Game 3 on Saturday.

Now that the Warriors find themselves in the uncomfortable position of being two losses away from an early vacation, Stephen Curry is calling Game 4 "obviously a must-win."

Curry, after struggling again in a second straight loss since winning the NBA's Most Valuable Player award, still recommends staying the course.

"Nobody is defeated in our locker room," said Curry, who scored a game-high 23 points but struggled to 2-for-10 shooting from 3-point range and committed four first-half turnovers. "Nobody is down.

"This is a big opportunity for us, a big challenge, and I like our chances."

The Warriors trailed by 19 points in the fourth quarter and blew chances to make the game closer before going on a late 11-2 run to cut the lead to four.

But Courtney Lee responded with a 3-pointer, and then with the shot clock expiring, Marc Gasol banked in a jumper with his foot on the 3-point line to push the Grizzlies' lead back to eight.

Zach Randolph led Memphis with 22 points, and Gasol added 21. The Grizzlies also got 22 points off 17 Warriors turnovers.

"That was a killer," said Warriors coach Steve Kerr, whose team committed 20 turnovers in the Game 2 loss. "It's the exact same story as the other night."

Said Curry: "We have to play better and play more under control and just be ourselves, and that's the challenge for us."

The Warriors came back from a 20-point deficit to win a first-round game against New Orleans. Over and over again, Memphis staved off the Warriors in front of a raucous crowd in the arena known as the Grindhouse despite Klay Thompson getting back on track with a 20-point performance and Harrison Barnes coming through with 16 points.

Thompson and Curry hit back-to-back 3-pointers to cut the deficit to 60-54 in the third quarter. But Thompson, who drew the defensive assignment on point guard Mike Conley, sat with four personal fouls with 6:21 left in the third. Andrew Bogut suffered the same fate.

The momentum was halted, and the Warriors began spinning their wheels.

With the Warriors trailing by nine points, they proceeded to commit three consecutive turnovers.

Draymond Green struggled once again as he was held to six points on 1-for-8 shooting and committed five turnovers. He threw another pass away after the Warriors hurriedly got the ball in bounds seeing that Gasol was momentarily shaken up on the other end of the court.

Center Festus Ezeli (31) and guard Stephen Curry (30) try to block the shot of the Grizzlies' Mike Conley, who was playing in his second game back since undergoing facial surgery. (AP Images)

After that one, Kerr buried his head in his hands.

"Again, some lack of poise, some critical turnovers that sort of stopped our momentum," Kerr said. "All those little mistakes, especially against a veteran team like Memphis, you're going to pay if you make them."

Then in the fourth, after Marreese Speights scored six straight points to pull the Warriors to within 13, he suffered a strained right calf and limped off to the locker room. He is unlikely to play in Game 4 and underwent an MRI exam, according to a Warriors source.

The Warriors found some success using a smaller lineup in the fourth and double-teaming the Grizzlies' big men.

"I think if we play the way we did the last four minutes defending the paint, we're going to win this series," Thompson said. "We made the adjustment. It was just too late."

The Warriors, with the highest-scoring offense in the NBA, went into halftime with only 39 points for a second straight game, as the Grizzlies led by 16. Only once in the regular season did Golden State score less than 40 in the first half. ∎

GAME 4
MAY 11, 2015 • MEMPHIS, TENNESSEE
WARRIORS 101, GRIZZLIES 84

RETURN TO FORM

CURRY SCORES 33, WARRIORS TAKE COMMAND EARLY TO EVEN SERIES

BY DIAMOND LEUNG

Stephen Curry was smiling again after putting together a playoff performance befitting his MVP status.

The Warriors gritted their teeth against the Memphis Grizzlies, resembling the team that had won 67 games in the regular season with hot shooting and a swarming defense.

And now that the Warriors evened up the Western Conference semifinals by walloping the Grizzlies 101-84 on Monday in Game 4, the momentum belongs to Golden State again.

Curry had 33 points, eight rebounds and five assists to shake off a mini-slump that happened to take place the same week he hoisted the MVP trophy. This time, Curry played so well that MVP chants could be heard in an emptying road arena, and a fan wearing a Grizzlies shirt high-fived the Warriors star.

"He was pumped up," Curry said, grinning. "He made the first move, right?"

It was the Warriors who were the aggressors as they avoided losing a third straight game for the first time this season. Curry caught fire, going 11 for 22 from the field, including 4 for 9 from 3-point range after not attempting a shot for the first eight minutes of the game.

"He was just trying to get the ball moving, which was our focus," Warriors coach Steve Kerr said. "I thought he was really patient early, and then the game came to him.

"Once we moved it a couple times and he got an open look, he got into better rhythm."

Said Memphis coach Dave Joerger: "The ball movement was excellent."

The Warriors led by 17 at halftime and built a 26-point lead in the third quarter on the back of consecutive 3-pointers from Curry, Klay Thompson and Andre Iguodala. They would finish 14 for 33 from long distance after consecutive games of being held to 6 for 26 from beyond the arc.

Draymond Green had 16 points, 10 rebounds and four assists, playing his way out of a rut. Thompson added 15 points, and Harrison Barnes came through with 12 points and six rebounds while holding his own against Zach Randolph. The Warriors won easily despite committing 21 turnovers while helping force 16 of them from Memphis.

Marc Gasol led the Grizzlies with 19 points, but they shot 37.5 percent from the field and got off to the slow start after Kerr made an adjustment.

Center Andrew Bogut was assigned to guard the Grizzlies' Tony Allen, who while forced out of the paint and to the perimeter finished 2 for 9 from the field. Bogut also added nine rebounds and four assists.

Stephen Curry goes to the hole during the 101-84 victory, which shifted the series' momentum back to Golden State. (AP Images)

"More than anything, it's just the attitude," Kerr said of the defense. "You're desperate when you're down 2-1 on the road, so there was a sense of urgency. We knew we had to compete every possession.

"I thought the first couple games our defense was decent but not playoff-level, not championship-level where you're competing every possession."

The Warriors got a lift from their two former All-Stars off the bench as well. Iguodala made three 3-pointers, and David Lee provided key minutes as one of the first players off the bench with big man Marreese Speights out because of a strained right calf.

The Warriors got off to quick start and took at 28-20 lead at the end of the first quarter as Curry beat the buzzer with his first 3-pointer of the game.

"We settled in and didn't force anything," Curry said.

"We set the tone in the first quarter and kept putting on the gas pedal the whole game, and that's how we play."

Green finished with seven turnovers and committed three first-half fouls but helped the Warriors' start by making his first four field goal attempts. ■

Above: Harrison Barnes, a starter after playing off the bench last season, slams home two of his 12 points in Game 4. (AP Images) Opposite: In a matchup between two of the best point guards in the West, Stephen Curry readies to cross over Mike Conley. (AP Images)

GAME 5
MAY 13, 2015 • OAKLAND, CALIFORNIA
WARRIORS 98, GRIZZLIES 78

ROARING AHEAD

STINGY WARRIORS HOLD GRIZZLIES UNDER 40 PERCENT SHOOTING

BY DIAMOND LEUNG

Blow by blow, the Warriors beat up Memphis with a barrage of backbreaking shots and now find themselves one win away from advancing to the Western Conference finals.

The Warriors crushed the Grizzlies 98-78 on Wednesday in Game 5 of the conference semifinals to take a 3-2 lead in the series as they could not be stopped at Oracle Arena.

Stephen Curry did a little bit of everything, racking up 18 points — all on 3-point shots — seven rebounds, six steals and five assists.

Klay Thompson scored a game-high 21 points, with his 4-point play in the fourth quarter giving the Warriors a 24-point lead and one more thrill to remember before they headed back to Memphis for Game 6.

"Why try to beat somebody at their game?" Warriors forward Draymond Green said. "We play our brand of basketball."

The defense smothered Memphis for the lowest point total for a Warriors playoff opponent in 40 years. Meanwhile, the Grizzlies were already in a bind when top perimeter defender Tony Allen was unable to play and guard Thompson due to a sore hamstring.

With Andre Iguodala (16 points) and Harrison Barnes (14 points) enjoying big games as well, there was little the Grizzlies could do but fight another day. Even if the Warriors can't close out the series on Friday, Memphis would have to win a Game 7 in Oakland to advance.

"You don't want to mess around," Warriors coach Steve Kerr said of looking to end the series in Game 6. "You never know what can happen."

If Game 5 wasn't the knockout blow, it sure felt like one. The Warriors' defense limited the Grizzlies to 39.8 percent shooting from the field. Marc Gasol led them with 18 points, but was 8 for 22 from the field with Green draped all over him.

Andrew Bogut added six points all on alley-oop dunks, nine rebounds and four blocked shots. Zach Randolph was held to two points after a hot first quarter.

"You figure out their moves," Green said of guarding the Grizzlies' big men. "It's just like wine. You're better with time."

The Warriors were 14 for 30 from 3-point range with Curry and Thompson combining for nine of the makes.

Curry erupted and hit four 3-pointers in the first quarter alone, bringing the Warriors back from as many as 13 points down to lead 26-25.

David Lee (left) and Draymond Green swarm to defend the Grizzlies' Kosta Koufos during the fourth quarter of Game 5. The Warriors held the Grizzlies to 39.8% shooting as they took a 3-2 series lead. (D. Ross Cameron/Staff)

Curry tantalized Beno Udrih with the dribble before launching from long range to close out the quarter with the Warriors in the middle of an 18-2 run. After the shot, Curry motioned to the Oracle crowd to get even louder than it already was. He hit two 3-pointers during that stretch, with Green adding a 3-point play.

Randolph had gotten the Grizzlies off to a hot start, making his first four field goal attempts including a rare 3-pointer to give them an 11-4 lead. He had nine of those points and four rebounds in the first four minutes.

While the Warriors blew numerous opportunities to score in transition and committed seven first-quarter turnovers, the Grizzlies took a 23-10 lead before Curry and Barnes led the comeback.

Barnes had a 3-pointer and a jumper followed by Curry's 3-pointer in transition to cut the deficit to 23-15. It was Barnes whose second 3-pointer gave the Warriors a 41-35 lead in the second quarter.

Thompson hit a 3-pointer, and then Curry drained his fifth from long range to give the Warriors a 49-37 lead. They finished the first half with 14 fast break points, with the Grizzlies failing to score any.

Barnes scored 10 points by halftime and despite committing four turnovers was aggressive and effective. Late in the second quarter, his foot slid while guarding Courtney Lee and caused him to painfully do the splits. He still came out to start the second half.

Curry's sixth 3-pointer gave the Warriors a 63-51 lead, jump-starting a 12-4 Warriors run. Iguodala had two dunks in transition off passes from Curry, who after the second one once again motioned for the crowd to go crazy.

"You see how many open looks we get just by being unselfish and trying to make the right play," Curry said. ■

Klay Thompson celebrates after hitting a 3-point basket in the fourth quarter. Thompson led the Warriors with 21 points. (Ray Chavez/Staff)

GAME 6

MAY 15, 2015 • MEMPHIS, TENNESSEE
WARRIORS 108, GRIZZLIES 95

WEST FINALS, HERE WE COME

STEPH CURRY SINKS 62-FOOTER TO END THIRD QUARTER

BY DIAMOND LEUNG

With a bang, the Warriors advanced to the Western Conference finals for the first time since 1976.

Stephen Curry sealed the semifinal series against Memphis with a 32-point performance in a 108-95 win in Game 6 on Friday, cutting down the Grizzlies' potential comeback with a stunning shot from three quarters of the way down the court.

The ball squirted to Curry off a blocked shot with one second left in the third quarter, and with a two-handed heave the ball traveled from inside one three-point line toward the other end of the court.

"I said, 'I think this is going in,'" Warriors coach Steve Kerr said.

Splash. From an estimated 62 feet away, the rainbow found nothing but net and gave Golden State an eight-point lead headed into the fourth.

"I was just like, 'That's the reason he's the MVP,'" Warriors forward Harrison Barnes said.

Said Memphis guard Mike Conley: "When he made it, it was kind of like, 'What happened?'"

The Grizzlies were sunk, as the Warriors followed with the first seven points of the fourth to push the lead back up to 83-68. Curry poured in three more 3-pointers in the final period to finish with eight of them and he added 10 assists and six rebounds.

The Warriors had gotten all they could handle with the Grizzlies' comeback attempt before Curry's prayer was answered. Jeff Green's jumper cut the Warriors' lead to 65-64 with 3:20 left in the third, as they were in trouble with Andrew Bogut and Draymond Green each on the bench with four fouls. But Andre Iguodala responded with two 3-pointers, and another substitute in Festus Ezeli had a dunk to extend the lead.

Curry's dagger sank hearts in Memphis, and now the Warriors will face the winner of the Houston Rockets-Los Angeles Clippers series.

"We're not done," Warriors center Andrew Bogut said. "We're not satisfied just to go the conference finals and go home. We want to the conference finals and win a championship."

Klay Thompson scored 20 points, and Draymond Green added 16 points and 12 rebounds.

Marc Gasol scored 21 points, and Zach Randolph added 15 for the Grizzlies. Vince Carter scored 16 points off the bench. But they never did get comfortable going

Stephen Curry has reason to celebrate. Not only did he connect on a 62-foot shot to end the third quarter, but his team also finished off the Grizzlies. (AP Images)

up against the Warriors' defense. The Grizzlies were held to 37.4 percent from the field.

The Warriors won the series not only by hitting jump shots but also displaying some of the grit-and-grind mentality that was a hallmark of their opponents. They came back from a one-game deficit in the series to win three straight including twice on the road.

"The Warriors used to have an M.O. of being a soft team, and I've noticed since I've been here that's something that we've always talked about changing, and we've changed that," Draymond Green said. "We feel like we can match up with anyone."

Golden State's defense wore down a Grizzlies team that never once scored 100 points in the series.

Then there was Curry, who went from singing the blues from long distance earlier in the series to going 8 for 13 in Game 6.

"The way he finished, that's all that matters," Harrison Barnes said. "He's the best closer there is."

The buzzer beater from past midcourt, the one Memphis coach Dave Joerger called "a shot to the gut," was one Curry had practiced.

"Every day," Curry said. "And that's not a lie."

The top-seeded Warriors improved to 53-0 this season after taking a 15-point lead in games, and they managed to extend it to that margin early against the Grizzlies.

Curry hit two 3-pointers, and Thompson had one of his own as part of a 9-0 run that gave the Warriors a 25-10 lead.

The Warriors shot 65 percent from the field in the first quarter, including 6 for 9 from 3-point range with Curry and Thompson each hitting three of them.

It didn't help the Grizzlies that top perimeter defender Tony Allen started the game on an injured hamstring and managed to play only five minutes in which he noticeably grimaced and did not return.

Unfortunately for the Grizzlies, each time they cut the deficit to single digits, the Warriors answered. Three times when the Warriors' lead was whittled to nine points, Shaun Livingston responded with baskets.

Courtney Lee banked in a jump shot at the buzzer to cut the Warriors' lead to 58-49 at halftime, but the Grizzlies never did take a lead in the game. ∎

Golden State Warriors center Andrew Bogut, left, celebrates with Festus Ezeli, right, after the Warriors beat the Memphis Grizzlies in Game 6. (AP Images)

GAME 1
MAY 19, 2015 • OAKLAND, CALIFORNIA
WARRIORS 110, ROCKETS 106

ONE THE HARD WAY

WARRIORS RALLY FROM 16 DOWN TO WIN GAME 1 IN WEST FINALS

BY DIAMOND LEUNG

The Warriors continued their dominance of the Houston Rockets this season with a 110-106 win in Game 1 of the Western Conference finals Tuesday.

To earn the playoff victory, Stephen Curry and the Warriors had to survive a showdown at home after sweeping the regular-season series.

Curry scored a game-high 34 points, hitting six 3-pointers to get the better of MVP runner-up James Harden, who took the game over at times and finished with 28 points.

The Warriors had the last laugh as they proceeded to go on an 11-0 run after Harden had tied the score at 97 with 5:28 left. Harrison Barnes had back-to-back dunks off an inbound pass and a putback. Then Curry found himself open for a layup under the basket and hit a 3-pointer.

Houston responded with a 9-0 run to cut the lead to two, but Curry calmly sank two free throws with 11.8 seconds left to seal the win in the Warriors' first conference finals game in 39 years.

"We expected it to be a battle," Curry said. "It wasn't going to be a blowout at all."

Curry was 6 for 11 from 3-point range, fending off the Rockets' challenges over and over again. Shaun Livingston added 18 points off the bench, speeding up the pace of the game to spark a second-quarter run that turned the tide. Draymond Green collected 13 points, 12 rebounds and eight assists while helping stop center Dwight Howard.

Harden poured in 21 of his points in the second half and finished with 11 rebounds and nine assists.

"He's hitting tough contested fall-away twos," Warriors coach Steve Kerr said. "There's not a whole lot you can do."

Harden took control for the Rockets as Howard missed much of the second half due to a knee bruise and was held to seven points and 13 rebounds.

The Warriors trailed by as many as 16 points in the second quarter. Then came their heavy-handed response to the Rockets, who entered the series with some momentum after coming back from a 3-1 deficit to win their Western Conference semifinal series against the Los Angeles Clippers.

Closing the first half on a 25-6 run, the Warriors erased the deficit and took a 58-55 halftime lead. Curry hit a step-back jumper at the buzzer to send them into the locker room with all the momentum.

That shot was actually the only one from Curry during the run, which was keyed by a switch the

Golden State's lockdown defender, Draymond Green, tries to contain James Harden, who had an excellent all-around game in the opener of the Western Conference Finals. (Doug Duran/Staff)

Warriors made on defense and contributions from the bench.

Green drew the assignment at center and bothered Howard after Andrew Bogut had picked up three fouls in seven minutes of action and finished the game scoreless.

Livingston scored 16 points in the first half, including eight of the Warriors' points on a 10-0 run to cut the lead.

"You can't give a really good shooting team easy layups, confidence, and that's what we did in the second quarter," Harden said.

The crowd noise at Oracle Arena was deafening as Green then drew an offensive foul on Howard and scored on a tip-in at the other end. Howard would commit five first-half turnovers.

"They struggled a bit with the small lineup when they were big with Dwight, and that's what kind of changed the game for us," Green said.

After Klay Thompson tied the score at 53 with a layup, the tidal wave continued as Barnes put the Warriors ahead with a 3-pointer.

"I'm proud of the way we stuck with it, and we became the aggressor in the second quarter," Curry said.

It was the Rockets who had gotten off to a hot start. They led 31-24 after the first quarter and successfully scored in transition on the Warriors. Josh Smith hit a 3-pointer and had a dunk in transition before Corey Brewer scored on a fast-break layup to cap a 9-0 run that gave the Rockets a 49-33 lead.

Howard didn't look the same after colliding with Smith in the first quarter. He limped around and briefly went back to the locker room, but the Warriors could not take advantage of his absence while the Rockets went on an 11-2 run.

Houston had led 9-2 before Thompson scored seven straight points to tie the score and hit his only 3-pointer of the game. ■

Stephen Curry, who scored 34 points, eludes Josh Smith (5) and James Harden (13) while driving to the basket. (Ray Chavez/Staff)

GAME 2
MAY 22, 2015 • OAKLAND, CALIFORNIA
WARRIORS 99, ROCKETS 98

GRAND THEFT

WARRIORS DENY HARDEN A FINAL SHOT, HOLD ON FOR 2-0 SERIES LEAD

BY DIAMOND LEUNG

Stephen Curry punched the air after having ended the cookout between him and James Harden.

Harden crumpled to the floor and buried his head, his last opportunity to win the game dashed by the Splash Brothers' defensive stand.

The Warriors edged the Houston Rockets in a wild 99-98 win in Game 2 of the Western Conference finals Thursday to take a 2-0 lead in the series. Curry in the end brought along a friend to the duel, as he and Klay Thompson forced a frenzied Harden to lose the ball just before the buzzer.

"The two guys who get a lot of credit for their offense made the best defensive play of the night," Warriors forward Draymond Green said.

"They call it a home run trot when you kind of jog back. That was a championship trot right there. Everybody sprinted back and got into position and made a play."

Harden scored a game-high 38 points, but Curry poured in 33 points and got the win after the Warriors had blown a 17-point first-half lead. The slugfest saw the top two finishers in the MVP race each go 13 for 21 from the field, but Harden's final charge was met with resistance.

Harden grabbed a rebound with 6.9 seconds left and immediately raced to other end of the court, but Curry and Thompson cut him off and surrounded him. The ball was fumbled away, leaving Harden on his knees exasperated that he wasn't able to attempt a potential game-winning shot.

"It's just don't let him get a shot off and try to be the hero," Curry said of the defense.

Harden knocked down a curtain in frustration on his way back to the locker room and later said, "It hurts, but they did what they had to do. They won two games at home."

The Rockets' Dwight Howard finished with 19 points and 17 rebounds, playing with a brace two days after spraining his left knee, but it wasn't enough as the Warriors brought muscle with them as well. Andrew Bogut at one point had his mouth bloodied by Howard on his way to collecting 14 points on 7-of-9 shooting, eight rebounds, five blocks and four assists. Green added 12 points, eight rebounds and seven assists.

"This was more of a street fight, more of a traditional game involving big guys protecting the rim and hard fouls and blocked shots," Warriors coach Steve Kerr said.

Curry and Harden provided the main event. Curry's stepback jumper gave the Warriors a 98-90 lead 1:39 left before Harden responded with six straight points. Pressure on Curry forced the Warriors into an

Klay Thompson (11) and Stephen Curry (30) force James Harden into the game-ending turnover, which sealed the victory for Golden State. (Nhat V. Meyer/Staff)

eight-second backcourt violation with the Warriors leading by three. Harden, for his ninth assist, tossed an alley-oop to Howard to cut the Warriors' lead to one point with 33 seconds left.

Curry dazzled with five 3-pointers. Harden fell one assist shy of a triple-double. The Warriors still improved to 6-0 this season against Houston.

"It doesn't matter if James has 40 or five (points)," said Thompson, who was 1 for 7 from 3-point range and among the Warriors to defend Harden. "It's whether we win or lose."

For a moment in the second quarter, Andre Iguodala delivered the powerful message that the Warriors were coming, and there was little the Rockets could do to stop them. He soared before throwing down a dunk off a stolen inbound pass. The hobbled Howard could only step aside at the sight of Iguodala elevating.

The slam was part of a 12-0 run that pushed the lead to 16 at a time in the game when Curry was on the bench and the Warriors' second unit took center stage. Harrison Barnes' 3-pointer pushed the lead to 17.

The Warriors moved to 54-0 this season when opening up leads of at least 15 points, but doing so wasn't easy. The Rockets erased the lead over the final seven minutes of the quarter as they closed the first half on a 23-6 run capped by an alley-oop to Howard that tied the score at 55. Harden scored 12 straight Rockets points at one point and then came out in the third quarter and hit a 3-pointer to give Houston its first lead.

The Rockets took a 65-59 lead before the Warriors responded with a 12-2 run highlighted by a monster dunk from Thompson and Curry hitting his fifth 3-pointer.

Given open looks, Curry was 4 for 6 from 3-point range in the first quarter to give the Warriors a 36-28 lead.

Seventeen Warriors turnovers enabled the Rockets to stay within striking distance, with seven of them coming in the first quarter due in large part to sloppy passing. Curry finished with six turnovers to go along with six assists.

"To be here sitting here 2-0, that's big because we've got to feel like that game is coming soon where we put it together," Green said. ∎

Harrison Barnes uses a nifty move around the basket to elude Dwight Howard, a stalwart shot blocker. (Nhat V. Meyer/Staff)

GAME 3
MAY 23, 2015 • HOUSTON, TEXAS
WARRIORS 115, ROCKETS 80

HOU-MILIATION

CURRY'S 40 POINTS PUT WARRIORS ONE WIN AWAY FROM NBA FINALS

BY DIAMOND LEUNG

Calmly removing his mouthpiece after a 3-pointer that broke the Houston Rockets' backs and hopes for a comeback, Stephen Curry stared into a crowd stunned into silence.

The fight is nearly over after Curry exploded for 40 points in the Warriors' 115-80 flogging of the demoralized Rockets on Saturday to take a 3-0 lead in the best-of-seven Western Conference finals.

Curry was dominant as he carried the Warriors to a hot start resulting in a 25-point halftime lead and eventual blowout that left them one win from advancing to the NBA Finals. He hit seven 3-pointers and had a stretch in the second quarter when he scored 14 of 16 of the Warriors' points to give his team a 20-point lead.

"Steph was Steph," Warriors coach Steve Kerr said. "He's the MVP."

In a game when Rockets fans showered James Harden with chants of "MVP" long after the race was decided, he was held to 17 points on 3-for-16 shooting. Houston had played the Warriors close when Harden was hot in the first two games of the series. This time, Harrison Barnes drew the challenging defensive assignment, and the Warriors notched their largest playoff win in the shot clock era.

"We seemed to get down because our offense wasn't flowing," Rockets coach Kevin McHale said.

Curry in contrast was 12 for 19 from the field, including a white-hot 7 for 9 from 3-point range. After Harden cut the lead to 18 points in the third quarter with a 3-pointer, Curry responded with one of his own from the corner as part of an 8-0 run before turning right around to the crowd to soak in the silence.

After a subsequent 3-pointer from the same corner pushed the lead to 31 points, he heard a four-letter word from a fan that he wouldn't repeat.

"That's the one I turned around and just kind of said, 'Sit down.'

"If they want to talk, hopefully they can take some back in my fashion."

Draymond Green collected 17 points, 13 rebounds and five assists while Klay Thompson had 17 points and five rebounds.

Josh Smith scored 16 points for Houston, and Dwight Howard added 14 points and 14 rebounds, but it was the Warriors who won the heavyweight battle and the battle of the boards by a 60-39 margin.

The most memorable of the rebounds came in the

Stephen Curry reacts after scoring one of his 12 buckets during his magnificent 40-point performance. (Nhat V. Meyer/Staff)

second quarter when Curry boxed out the 6-foot-11 Howard, corralled the ball with one arm and drew a shooting foul on the putback attempt.

"Big Fella Curry," Ezeli said, calling out to Curry in the locker room. "That was a huge play for us."

Andrew Bogut scored 10 of his 12 points in the first quarter and grabbed 12 rebounds while Ezeli had 10 points and six rebounds.

"We can't fold," said Howard, whose team lost three straight games for the first time this season. "We can't quit because we're down. It's easy to just give up and say, 'They're playing great.' It's easy to do that. But they're going to have to take all of us out on a stretcher.

"We ain't going down like that. I mean, we've got to fight for our lives."

The Warriors believed they had not played their best while taking a 2-0 lead in the series. So they set the tone in a first quarter highlighted by strong displays of ball movement and defense.

They didn't have a single turnover in the quarter, and the only one committed in the half came on an illegal screen from Barnes. The Rockets shot only 29.3 percent from the field in the first half.

"It's a great lesson for our team," Kerr said. "If we defend like crazy and take care of the ball, we're going to be in good shape."

Added Green: "We said coming on the road in order to win against this team, we knew we couldn't turn the ball over. It fuels their crowd, and they'll get threes off turnovers that fuels their crowd as well."

The Rockets were 5 for 25 from 3-point range, and by the fourth quarter, the Toyota Center crowd began emptying.

It was the Warriors making all the noise. ∎

Stephen Curry smiles toward the Toyota Center crowd after connecting on a 3-pointer, one of seven he made during the blowout victory. (Jose Carlos Fajardo/Staff)

GAME 4
MAY 25, 2015 • HOUSTON, TEXAS
ROCKETS 128, WARRIORS 115

COULD HAVE BEEN WORSE

MISERABLE START, CURRY'S CHILLING FALL TOO MUCH TO OVERCOME

BY DIAMOND LEUNG

After Stephen Curry fell and hit his head on the court, he was down for a few minutes and then remained in the locker room for about a quarter before making his return.

The Warriors' comeback, on the other hand, fell short. The Houston Rockets staved off elimination with a 128-115 win Monday in Game 4 of the Western Conference finals, sending the series back to Oakland with the Warriors leading 3-1.

"I tried to do what I could to get my team back in the game," Curry said. "We came up a little short, but we'll be all right next game."

Forty years to the day the Warriors won their last NBA championship, advancing to the NBA Finals wasn't to be, as Houston star James Harden scored 45 points. The Rockets seized control of the game with a hot start and led by as many as 25 points.

Then Curry was upended as he leaped to defend a shot and was surrounded by his concerned teammates after his hard landing. He hit a 3-pointer to cut the Houston lead to 104-98 with 8:24 left, but Harden responded with seven straight points to start the Rockets' 10-0 run.

The Warriors got no closer than that despite Curry and Klay Thompson hitting six 3-pointers apiece. Harden answered with seven shots from long distance.

Thompson finished with 24 points, while Curry had 23 and Draymond Green added 21 points and 15 rebounds before fouling out.

The Rockets throttled the Warriors in the first quarter and took a 45-22 lead. The Warriors surrendered the most points of any quarter this season.

"That's ridiculous," Thompson said.

Houston raced out to a 12-0 lead as the Warriors missed their first five field goals and committed two turnovers in that stretch.

Josh Smith scored 13 of his 20 points in the quarter, making all three 3-point attempts. A 3-pointer from Harden pushed the lead to 20. The Rockets finished the quarter 17 for 22 from the field, including 8 for 9 from 3-point range.

"They won the game in the first quarter," Warriors coach Steve Kerr said. "They were ready to play, probably more ready than we were. We were on our heels. They were making shots from all over.

"We fought, but that game was a first-quarter game."

Draymond Green, the versatile forward who put up 21 points and 15 rebounds, tries to shrug off the Game 4 loss. (Jose Carlos Fajardo/Staff)

Then the Warriors experienced their most frightening moment of the season. Curry, the NBA's Most Valuable Player, was injured after going for a Trevor Ariza pump fake and going head over heels. The fall caused Curry's head to hit the court, and according to the team, he suffered a contusion.

"That was the scariest (fall)," Curry said. "You're in the air for a long time not knowing how you're going to hit the floor.

"It was just a scary feeling."

Kerr joined Curry's teammates and medical personnel in surrounding the point guard, who was down near the baseline. In the crowd, his wife and mother locked arms and held hands. Curry eventually was helped to the locker room as the Warriors trailed 55-36 with 5:52 left in the first half.

"It was nerve-racking because he wasn't moving. He was laying face down," Warriors forward Harrison Barnes said.

"Until he turned over, you're holding your breath."

An emotional Warriors team in his absence proceeded to start a comeback as Thompson, who struggled mightily on both ends of the court to start the game, stepped forward.

Thompson drained four 3-pointers in the next four minutes before halftime as the Warriors rallied to cut the deficit to 69-59. In the locker room, they were relieved to see Curry was walking around and appearing fine.

When Curry returned to the game with 5:58 left in the third, he air-balled his first shot and then had a 3-point attempt blocked. He finished 7 for 18 from the field, including 6 for 13 from 3-point range in 31 minutes.

Harden was 13 for 22 from the field, going 7 for 11 from 3-point range and adding nine rebounds and five assists.

The Rockets shot 56.6 percent from the field and scored 27 fast-break points.

"We got beat on backdoor cuts," Kerr said. "That's usually a pretty good sign that you're not ready to play defense. We got lost a couple times in transition. There were some signs early on that we were not sharp." ∎

Stephen Curry takes a horrific spill after going for a Trevor Ariza pump fake, though the NBA MVP returned to the game with 5:58 left in the third quarter. (Nhat V. Meyer/Staff)

GAME 5
MAY 27, 2015 • OAKLAND, CALIFORNIA
WARRIORS 104, ROCKETS 90

40-YEAR WAIT IS OVER

WARRIORS ARE BOUND FOR NBA FINALS AFTER BARNES KEYS FOURTH-QUARTER RUN

BY DIAMOND LEUNG

After 40 years of suffering and waiting, the Warriors are back in the NBA Finals.

Confetti rained down on Oracle Arena after they became Western Conference champions, having defeated the Houston Rockets 104-90 on Wednesday to claim a 4-1 semifinal series victory.

Yet in the locker room, there wasn't much celebrating.

"We're not satisfied at all," Draymond Green explained.

"It'll be way different if we get four more wins."

The Warriors, who will face LeBron James and the Cleveland Cavaliers in the NBA Finals, punched their ticket after Stephen Curry scored 26 points and Harrison Barnes poured it on in the fourth quarter to finish with 24 points.

Curry came through after suffering a head contusion in his previous game, and did so while sore and wearing a protective shooting sleeve. Klay Thompson added 20 points before getting kneed in the head and after the game experiencing concussion-like symptoms.

"We're four wins away from the goal," Curry told the crowd at Oracle Arena, which cheered so loudly that his words could hardly be heard.

"Hey, why not us?"

The Warriors, who went to the postseason in only three of the previous 20 seasons before hiring rookie coach Steve Kerr, will host Game 1 of the NBA Finals on June 4. Kerr is back after winning five NBA championships as a player.

"It's maybe even more rewarding, because you feel responsible for a lot of people's welfare and happiness," Kerr said.

"They're an incredible group, and it's extremely gratifying to be a part of it."

Rockets guard James Harden was held to 14 points on 2-for-11 shooting and suffered the indignity of committing an NBA playoff-record 13 turnovers, a number the MVP runner-up said was "unacceptable." Dwight Howard led the Rockets with 18 points and 16 rebounds, but they shot only 35.1 percent from the field.

"We're a jump-shooting team that didn't shoot well," Green said, jabbing those who had labeled the Warriors as such, after a game they won while shooting 40.7 percent. "We're actually pretty good on the defensive end, too."

Barnes noted that late in the game he was playing alongside Green and Festus Ezeli, who had 12 points and nine rebounds off the bench. All three were

Warriors fans at Oracle Arena celebrate as Stephen Curry leaves the court after Golden State's 104-90 win over Houston in Game 5 of the Western Conference Finals. (Nhat V. Meyer/Staff)

products of a 2012 draft class that has made three straight playoff appearances.

Barnes scored nine straight Warriors points on a jumper, 3-pointer, runner and dunk to give his team an 87-72 lead with 7:10 left.

The outburst came immediately after the Warriors saw Thompson leave for the locker room bleeding from an ear laceration after getting kneed in the head by the Rockets' Trevor Ariza.

When the Rockets cut the Warriors' lead to eight points with 4:19 left, Barnes hit two free throws and ran the floor for another dunk.

The Warriors led 74-65 after a 7-0 run capped off by Curry's 3-pointer and a dunk from Andre Iguodala, who had stolen the ball for Harden's 11th turnover that tied the NBA playoff record. The assist came from Green, who started the game 1 for 10 from the field but contributed on the defensive end as well.

"To get to the Finals, first time in 40 years for the Warriors, it's more than relief," Kerr said. "It's joy.

"I'm happy for everybody, especially our fans. Forty years is a long time."

Jason Terry scored seven straight Rockets points before the Warriors' run.

Thompson scored the first five points of the second half to push the Warriors' lead to 57-46. But he would soon be forced to the bench after committing his fourth and fifth fouls only 22 seconds apart. The Rockets responded with an 8-0 run capped off by Ariza's steal in the backcourt and 3-point play.

The Warriors led 52-46 at halftime, with Barnes and Curry hitting back-to-back 3-pointers to push their first-half lead to as many as eight points.

Harden was held to 11 points while committing eight turnovers in the half, as Andre Iguodala came off the bench to guard him.

Thompson caught fire in the second quarter, hitting three 3-pointers in a row to spark a 13-2 run that gave the

Stephen Curry, who had a game-high 26 points, drives to the hoop past veteran Jason Terry. (Ray Chavez/Staff)

Warriors a 30-24 lead. He hit his sixth shot in a row with a dunk in transition off a missed Harden 3-point attempt and Curry's rebound and quick pass.

The Rockets led 22-17 after the first quarter as the Warriors got off to another slow start, committing six turnovers and going 1 for 8 from 3-point range.

Howard in the quarter collected eight points, five rebounds and two blocked shots. Andrew Bogut also committed two of his fouls and had to take a seat on the bench.

The Warriors started the game 1 for 9 from the field as the Rockets jumped out to an 8-2 lead.

Bouncing back, the Warriors took back the lead after Curry stole the ball from Harden and Thompson made a reverse layup in transition to give them a 10-9 lead.

Harden hit all seven of his free throws in the quarter, stretching out the Rockets' lead to 20-12. ∎

Above: Sweetie, a 106-year-old fan, reacts as she watches the Warriors game at her home surrounded by family and friends in the East Bay on May 27, 2015. (Josie Lepe/Staff) Opposite: the Golden State Warriors celebrate after winning Game 5 to return the franchise to the NBA Finals for the first time since 1975. (Doug Duran/Staff)

Warriors guard Stephen Curry holds up the NBA Most Valuable Player Trophy after being presented the award before Game 2 of the Western Conference Semifinals. (Jane Tyska/Staff)